THE CENTERS OF CIVILIZATION SERIES

BOSTON

In the Age of John Fitzgerald Kennedy

BOSTON

IN THE AGE OF
JOHN FITZGERALD
KENNEDY

By Walter Muir Whitehill

UNIVERSITY OF OKLAHOMA PRESS : NORMAN

By Walter Muir Whitehill

Spanish Romanesque Architecture of the Eleventh Century (London, 1941)

Fleet Admiral King (with Ernest J. King) (New York, 1952)

Boston Public Library: A Centennial History (Cambridge, Mass., 1956)

Boston: A Topographical History (Cambridge, Mass., 1959)

Independent Historical Societies (Boston, 1962)

Boston in the Age of John Fitzgerald Kennedy (Norman, 1966)

Library of Congress Catalog Card Number: 66-10289

Copyright 1966 by the University of Oklahoma Press, Publishing Division of the University. Composed and printed at Norman, Oklahoma, U.S.A., by the University of Oklahoma Press. First edition, February, 1966; second printing, June, 1966.

TO

JANE REVERE COOLIDGE WHITEHILL

"MY BEST HERITAGE

FROM THE

CITY OF HER FATHERS"

as M. A. DeWolfe Howe said of his wife
in the dedication of
Boston, the Place and the People
more than sixty years ago

Preface

IN THE LATE TWENTIES, soon after the appearance of Katherine Mayo's *Mother India*, an outraged resident of Calcutta published a scathing rejoinder, entitled *Uncle Sham*. This depressing record of murder, arson, rape, thievery, and other forms of vice and corruption, was carefully and conscientiously documented from contemporary American newspapers. While the era of Calvin Coolidge had many unlovely aspects, not the least of which was Prohibition, the picture presented by the author of *Uncle Sham* was far from correct, for he had drawn his conclusions entirely from printed sources, at a great distance, without personal observation.

If a resident of Calcutta were to judge present-day Boston solely on the evidence of newspaper headlines, he might readily conclude that it was a pretty sordid and depressing place. The *Boston Herald* in the first fortnight of August, 1963, offered its readers the following headlines on three different days: "BLAST AT D.P.W. SHOCKS STATE—Blatnick Probers Find Political 'Cesspool,' Charge Road Collusion Extended to Top"; "A Sorry Tale of Thievery, Cheating, Loose Management—NEW CHARGES ROCK GARAGE —Buckley Audit Reveals Gross Inefficiency"; "McGINNIS, TWO B & M AIDS INDICTED IN $75,000 CAR SALE 'KICKBACK'—U.S. Accuses Benson, Buyer." These refer, respectively, to the State Department of Public Works highway program, to the recently completed underground Boston Common Garage, and to the conduct of officers of the Boston and Maine Railroad. This was not a unique fortnight by any means. The spring of 1964 was adorned by a flowering of indictments of public officials. If the hypothetical resident of Calcutta were then to learn that the Peabody Museum of Salem has among its extensive collection of Liverpool ware pottery a jug inscribed "SUCCESS TO THE CROOKED BUT INTERESTING TOWN OF BOSTON," he might conclude that the political corruption of Boston had been well known in English ports in the early nineteenth century and that twentieth-century Bostonians gloried in it today by buying Wedgwood reproductions of this jug.

Now the jug was simply ordered in Liverpool by a Boston shipmaster out of affection for his home port, the "crooked" referring to nothing more than the street pattern of the town. Yet in recent years Boston has been crooked and narrow in more ways than one likes to realize. In an excellent article in the *Saturday Evening Post* of June 5, 1965, entitled "Massachusetts: Rogues and Reformers in a State on Trial," Edward R. F. Sheehan remarked that "the state's record of exposed corruption is unmatched, not only for its scope but for its ingenuity and its flamboyance." He pointed out what is all too familiar to readers of Boston newspapers, that in the preceding two years persons as highly placed as a former governor, two former speakers of the House of Representatives, two members of the Executive Council, and the former head of the state police "have been indicted or convicted on charges ranging from conspiracy to solicitation of bribes." Nevertheless, the vast majority of Bostonians live honest lives, while some at least apply excellent minds to high purposes. Even in the body politic Mr. Sheehan points out that Massachusetts is changing, that "the corruption so notorious now is essentially the sickness of a dying system," and that "the fragmented society is mending, however slowly."

Fifty years ago my schoolroom was decorated with likenesses of the bearded Homer and Euripides and the equally bearded Longfellow, Lowell, and Whittier, thus indicating to the young that Boston, as well as Greece, had its poets. In the middle of the nineteenth century Boston had indeed a substantial number of literary men—Emerson, Thoreau, Longfellow, Lowell, Whittier, Holmes, Prescott, Ticknor, Motley, and Parkman. The combination was so remarkable that the terms "Augustan Age" and "Golden Age" were commonly applied by devout admirers.

The Centers of Civilization Series of the University of Oklahoma Press is devoted to "cities, which from the earliest times to the present, have exercised a radiating influence upon the civilization in which they have existed." Many of the titles published and announced deal with the remote past—Thebes in the Eighteenth Dynasty, Athens in the Age of Pericles, Rome in the Augustan Age, Constantinople in the Age of Justinian, Florence in the Age of Dante. When Savoie Lottinville asked me to do a volume on Boston, I assumed that he had in mind an account of the city when Emerson and his contemporaries were abroad in the streets. The idea did not greatly appeal to me, for fundamentally I care more about the present and future of Boston than its past. Moreover, Van Wyck Brooks, M. A. De Wolfe Howe, Perry

Miller, F. O. Matthiessen, and a variety of literary critics had excavated the site to the point of diminishing returns.

For some days I compared the city of the mid-nineteenth century with the one around me. The latter was bigger, uglier, less homogeneous, yet it was far richer in the elements of civilization. In this past hundred years Harvard had changed from a country college to a great university; new institutions of learning had sprung up by the dozens. There were more books, more pictures, better music, without forgetting an abundance of Greek vases, Chinese and Egyptian sculpture, Japanese painting, and any number of things that were completely unavailable a century ago. Scientific research and experimentation had multiplied in every direction. Indeed, Alfred North Whitehead, addressing the American Academy of Arts and Sciences in 1942, had observed: "In so far as the world of learning today possesses a capital city, Boston with its various neighboring institutions approximates to the position that Paris occupied in the Middle Ages"; testimony, it should be remembered, not from an indulgent native son, but from a British philosopher of international experience and distinction, drawn to Boston in retirement by its galaxy of institutions.

It therefore became clear to me that, if Boston were to be included in the Centers of Civilization Series, the volume must deal with the present rather than the past. Savoie Lottinville agreed. Thus I attempt a portrait of the city around me in the nineteen sixties.

But it is no more good to call such a volume a "present-day portrait" than to describe a building as an example of "modern architecture." Modernity evaporates overnight. The "present" has slipped into the past long before the manuscript is typed, much less printed. The lifetime of a great man, known to every literate person, is a surer point of reference. When I began this book, a native Bostonian was President of the United States. He was the first since John Quincy Adams, for nobody could claim that Calvin Coolidge, although twice governor of Massachusetts, was other than a Vermonter—a good thing to be, but not the same thing. Many of us rejoiced in the vision, literacy, imagination, and energy that John F. Kennedy brought to his high office. Since November 22, 1963, his stature has not decreased, nor does it show greater likelihood of doing so than that of his predecessor who was similarly assassinated ninety-eight years earlier. In this Centers of Civilization Series, Pericles, Augustus, and Justinian were chosen as the points of reference for the volumes dealing with Athens, Rome, and Constantinople. When the British government chooses to devote to the memory of a Bostonian a portion of the green meadows of Runnymede, where King John signed the Magna Charta in 1215, it is, at least to me, obvious that this book should be entitled "Boston in the Age of John Fitzgerald Kennedy."

I was born in Cambridge sixty years ago. Save for nine years in Europe and for four of wartime service in the Naval Reserve, I have stuck closely to Boston. For the past nineteen years I have been based in the Boston Athenaeum, with some part-time teaching in Harvard College and with ties with a number of libraries and other institutions concerned with history and the arts. This book is consequently a somewhat personal one, in that, having deliberately returned to Boston after long absences, I naturally emphasize those elements in the city that have made it seem to me a desirable place to live. A scientist would write a different book; a businessman another. Each man chooses in the city what attracts him. Perhaps the clearest testimony that Boston is a center of civilization is the number of people who come to it from other parts of the country for some professional study and choose to remain permanently, as well as those, like Alfred North Whitehead, who come in retirement, or those like myself who, having grown up here, are drawn back.

The first three chapters attempt to explain how the city became what it is; the others briefly describe some of the institutions that, in my view, make it a center of civilization. Samuel Eliot Morison recently gave the title *One Boy's Boston* to the account of the first fourteen years of his life. This book is quite as much one man's Boston.

WALTER MUIR WHITEHILL

Boston Athenaeum
June 25, 1965

Contents

BOSTON
In the Age of John Fitzgerald Kennedy

I

The First Coming

READERS OF OTHER VOLUMES IN THIS SERIES will have noted how civilizations have flowered from the unlikely seeds of migrations and invasions. People mill about continents, cross mountains or seas, and eventually settle down. A sack of mixed seed scattered over a field may produce nourishment, beauty, or useless weeds. Some plants spring up to die in the autumn. Others prove to be perennial, while some grow into mighty trees. By selection and nurturing, new and more beautiful plants may evolve. So the seemingly random movements of peoples eventually produce settlements, some of which grow into cities that may, by a special combination of circumstances, become centers of civilization.

The migrations and cross-fertilizations that produced these centers in Europe stretched over centuries, with beginnings that are undocumented. Similar elements were involved in the evolution of Boston, but here the time is shorter—three and one-third centuries—and the migrants are easy to identify. Thus Boston offers a modern microcosm of the process.

The site of Boston was, in the early seventeenth century, a hilly peninsula, almost completely surrounded by water, overlooking a deep and well protected harbor. The chief record of its prehistory is an Indian fish weir, probably of about 1700 B.C., but with that we are hardly concerned, for Indians had no hand in the evolution of the city. There were only a few of them about, and those that there were scarcely mattered one way or the other. The history of Boston is one of successive European migrations and of what those peoples did in their new home.

The first to come were Puritan Englishmen of the Massachusetts Bay Company who arrived in 1630. For reasons of religion they had put the Atlantic Ocean between themselves and the Church of England as represented by King Charles I and by William Laud, Bishop of London, soon to become Archbishop of Canterbury. Since it was chartered ostensibly for commercial purposes, like the East India, the Muscovy, and other trading companies, it was assumed that the Bay Company's headquarters would be in London. But the Massachusetts Bay Company, under the leadership of its governor, John Winthrop, quietly moved—lock, stock, and barrel—to New England, bringing along its charter, which it proceeded to regard as authorization to set up a self-governing settlement in the wilderness.

The Puritans of the Massachusetts Bay Company had no notion of creating a maritime community when they arrived. Their motives in migrating were to found a church and state in which they might live according to their interpretation of the Word of God. In theory the fur trade would provide them with a means of support; in practice such beaver as there were soon ran out, leaving only farming and cattle-raising in the rocky soil of New England. During the great Puritan emigration following 1633, when newcomers were constantly arriving, bringing English goods and requiring food, those

4

who were earlier on the spot found a ready market for their corn and cattle.

But within a decade all that changed. Governor John Winthrop stated the dilemma with lucid simplicity in his journal for June 2, 1641: "The parliament of England setting upon a general reformation both of church and state, the Earl of Strafford being beheaded, and the archbishop (our great enemy) and many others of the great officers and judges, bishops and others, imprisoned and called to account, this caused all men to stay in England in expectation of a new world, so as few coming to us, all foreign commodities grew scarce, and our own of no price. Corn would buy nothing; a cow which cost last year £20 might now be bought for 4 or £5, etc., and many gone out of the country, so as no man could pay his debts, nor the merchants make return into England for their commodities, which occasioned many there to speak evil of us. These straits set our people on work to provide fish, clapboards, plank, etc., and to sow hemp and flax (which prospered very well) and to look out to the West Indies for a trade for cotton."

Thus New Englanders became shipbuilders, seamen, merchants, and fishermen. As Samuel Eliot Morison puts it: "Massachusetts went to sea, then, not of choice, but of necessity. Yet the transition was easy and natural. 'Farm us!' laughed the waters of the Bay in May-time to a weary yeoman, victim of the 'mocking spring's perpetual loss.' 'Here thou may'st reap without sowing—yet not without God's blessing; 'twas the Apostles' calling.'"

The Shawmut peninsula, upon which Boston was settled,

was an ideal setting for a seaport. It stood at the head of a sheltered deep-water harbor. It was connected on the south with the Roxbury mainland by a narrow neck (along the line of the present Washington Street) that only just prevented Boston from being an island. To the west of the neck great reaches of mud flats and salt marshes, covered by the tides at high water, were known as the Back Bay; beyond this the Charles River flowed down to the peninsula, dividing it from the mainland on the north and east as it approached Boston Harbor. On the east the peninsula fronted on the harbor, with the deep indentation of a cove that divided the town into North and South Ends. The considerable extent of shore line, only a few minutes' walk from any part of the peninsula, provided ample space for wharves and shipyards. Boston was, indeed, as William Wood described it in 1634 in his *New England Prospects*, "fittest for such as can Trade into England, for such commodities as the Countrey wants, being the chiefe place for shipping, and Merchandize."

John Josselyn, who spent the years 1663 to 1671 in New England, in describing Boston observed: "The houses are for the most part raised on the Sea-Banks and wharfed out with great industry and cost, many of them standing upon piles, close together on each side of the streets as in London, and furnished with many fair shops, their materials are Brick, Stone, Lime, handsomely contrived, with three meeting Houses or Churches, and a Town-house built upon pillars where the Merchants may confer, in the Chambers above they keep their monthly Courts."

It was, in short, an English town, a microcosm of the city of London on a tiny scale, for close ties of family and trade

6

linked Boston and London, as one may see in Bernard Bailyn's *The New England Merchants of the Seventeenth Century*. The few seventeenth-century houses that survived long enough to be engraved, as objects of antiquarian wonder, were generally small, with overhanging upper stories and numerous gables, in the crowded late-medieval English tradition. But the great three-story, free-standing brick house built by Peter Sargeant in 1679, which in 1716 became the residence of the governors of the province of Massachusetts Bay, was on a far ampler scale. Such a building as the Province House, coming only half a century after the first settlement of Boston, speaks eloquently of the success of trade.

For over fifty years Boston was a homogeneous Puritan community, in which the leaders of the Massachusetts Bay Company did what they had a mind to. Charles I was too occupied with Parliament and Scots to worry greatly about this remote settlement. As Parliament and Puritans triumphed over King and Church of England, the settlers of Boston came into a new relation with the homeland they had left. No longer were they a religious minority at odds with the government. Instead they found their relatives and co-religionists coming to occupy powerful places in England, so that in the sixteen forties and fifties men moved back and forth between England and New England in a manner that would hardly have been anticipated when the Massachusetts Bay Company settlers arrived in 1630. After the Restoration things were different. As Boston merchants prospered, London became increasingly aware of the existence of Massachusetts Bay. Yet it was only at the end of Charles II's reign that positive steps were taken to assert royal authority here. Thus

7

a Bible Commonwealth, substantially independent of England, flourished for half a century in the Massachusetts Bay.

The original Puritan clergy were in Anglican orders, but as the Massachusetts churches were organized on the Congregational principle, by which each group governed its own affairs, there was no truck with the Church of England. The First Church, which adopted its covenant on July 30, 1630, as the town grew was joined by others. A Second Church was established in the North End in 1650; a Third—the Old South—in the South End in 1669. When the peace of Zion was disturbed by religious discord, the dissenters and troublemakers were given short shrift. Roger Williams moved on to Rhode Island; Anne Hutchinson, the ring-leader of the Antinomian controversy, was duly banished from the colony. Quakers, who, unlike present-day Friends, were frequently disturbers of the peace, were chased out, and, if they persistently returned, hanged for their pains. Although the unwelcome Baptists, who organized themselves in Charlestown in 1665, built a meeting house in Boston in 1679—conveniently close to the mill pond—the first half-century of Boston was a scarcely disputed theocracy in which the three Puritan churches accounted for almost all the organized religion. For this period Boston Puritans were as little affected by the Church of England as they were by the home government.

This was too good to last, and it did not last because the growing prosperity of Boston trade made the place the subject of greater interest in England than it had been in the poorer and earlier decades. In 1684 the charter of Massachusetts Bay was declared null and void by Charles II; two years later royal authority was definitely established in Boston. Thus in May,

8

1686, there arrived, among other unwelcome visitors, the Reverend Robert Ratcliffe, M.A., an Anglican clergyman appointed by the Bishop of London to officiate in Boston according to the *Book of Common Prayer*. On December 20, 1686, Sir Edmund Andros, "in a Scarlet Coat, Laced," became the first royal governor of the Province of Massachusetts Bay. The Puritan isolation was over. Anglican services were held first in the Town House, then, to the disgust of its rightful congregation, in the Old South Church. Finally in 1689 a modest King's Chapel, built in one corner of the old burying ground at Tremont and School streets, was opened for Anglican worship. The growth of the Church of England in Boston during the first half of the eighteenth century is best indicated by the establishment of two new parishes—Christ Church, Salem Street, in the North End in 1723, and Trinity Church, Summer Street, in the South End in 1733—and by the need in mid-century of replacing the 1689 King's Chapel with the present stone building, designed by Peter Harrison.

Although the Congregational clergy—particularly Mathers—still made themselves heard, with a royal governor in residence and the Church of England on the scene, the lines of authority had altered. At the very time that men were growing richer, they found themselves subject to weaker Puritan restraints. Note, for example, Samuel Sewall's recorded disgust with the behavior of the rich merchant Samuel Shrimpton, his Anglican crony Captain Lidget, and others, who "came in a Coach from Roxbury about 9 aclock or past, singing as they came, being inflamed with Drink. At Justice Morgan's they stop and drink Healths, curse, swear, talk profanely and baudily to the great disturbance of the Town and grief of good people. Such high-handed wickedness has hardly been heard of before in Boston."

It was heard of again, for under the new regime Bostonians with money in their pockets used it much as an Englishman might at home. Thus Daniel Neal, in his *History of New England*, published in London in 1725, wrote: "Conversation in Boston is as polite as in most of the Cities and Towns in England, many of their Merchants having travell'd into Europe, and those that stay at home having the advantage of free Conversation with Travellers; so that a Gentleman from London would almost think himself at home at Boston, when he observes the numbers of people, their Houses, their Furniture, their Tables, their Dress and Conversation, which, perhaps, is as splendid and showy, as that of the most considerable Tradesmen in London."

Bernard Bailyn in his *Massachusetts Shipping, 1697–1714* points out that at the end of the seventeenth century Boston's fleet of seagoing vessels ranked third in size in the English-speaking world, being exceeded only by those of London and Bristol. "But [he writes] Boston alone of the Massachusetts port towns compared favorably with the English outports; the rest of the Colony's shipping communities appear as insignificant coastal villages when placed against the scale of British towns. In numbers of vessels Salem, the second Massachusetts port, would have ranked 39th among the 79 English towns that claimed any shipping at all and 31st in tonnage." Thus one sees that Boston was, as Carl Bridenbaugh points out, not a frontier town but a "city in the wilderness." And it was predominantly a seaport for its first century and a half.

From Captain John Bonner's map of 1722—the first to be engraved and published—one sees how the Long Wharf, which extended the present State Street into the middle of the Town Cove, served as the principal approach from the sea. At the intersection of State Street with what is now Washington Street—the only access from the land—stood the Town House (replaced after a fire of 1711 by the present brick Old State House) and the First Church. This site, where the roads from the sea and the mainland met, was the heart of the colonial town. On either side of the Town Cove were the regions known as the North and South Ends. The North End, where merchants "wharfed-out" before their houses until the shore became a continuous strip of wharves and shipyards, was the most populous and the saltiest. The South End too had its wharves, but it was, by comparison, a relatively open area of large houses, fields, pastures, and gardens, with ample space for the cumbersome ropewalks that provided cordage for Boston ships. To the west lay the forty-five acres of Boston Common, above which rose the three peaks of the Trimountain, the most conspicuous feature of the peninsula. These slopes and the West End behind them long remained open country.

If one had no other documents on colonial Boston, the crowded shore line of Bonner's 1722 map alone would testify to the predominantly maritime character of the place, for a town of twelve thousand inhabitants with upwards of forty wharves, more than a dozen shipyards and six ropewalks, could only be a thriving seaport. It was not only that, but the largest town in British North America—a place that it continued to hold until the middle of the eighteenth century, when it fell behind the faster growing ports of Philadelphia and New York. From 1630 to 1750 the pattern was one of steadily increasing growth; in the third quarter of the eighteenth century the curve went down, in no small part because of the political uncertainties and commotions that led to the American Revolution.

It is needless to repeat here the familiar story of the decade preceding the actual outbreak of hostilities. It was an unhappy time of honest but irreconcilable differences between native-born New Englanders. With fighting at Lexington and Concord on April 19, 1775, and at Bunker Hill on June 17, the die was cast. When Washington's army besieged the British in Boston the following winter, normal life was suspended. On March 17, 1776, impelled by Washington's artillery on Dorchester Heights, British troops and officials left, accompanied by many loyal supporters of the crown, including the Reverend Henry Caner, rector of King's Chapel, who took with him the church silver and records. In the Register of Marriages, he subsequently wrote the following entry: "An unnatural Rebellion of the Colonies against his Majesties Government obliged the Loyal Part of his subjects to evacuate their Dwellings and Substance, and to take refuge in Halifax, London, and elsewhere; by which means the public worship at King's Chapel became suspended, and is likely to remain so, till it shall please God in the Course of his Providence to change the hearts of the Rebels, or give Success to his Majesties arms for suppressing the Rebellion."

The hearts of the rebels remained unchanged and his Majesty's arms unsuccessful. The occupants of thirty of the seventy-three pews in King's Chapel sharing Dr. Caner's

12

sentiments went with him, most of them never to return. So it was in other parts of the town. A sizable number of Bostonians, including some of the most stylish, decamped entirely, leaving places to be filled by new men often risen from the obscurity of the farm by way of revolutionary military or political service, or through successful ventures at sea. Before John Adams went to Harvard College in 1751, no Adams had shown his face conspicuously outside of Braintree; from his time to the present, generation after generation, the family has maintained an extraordinary level of national distinction. Similarly, most of the names that we particularly associate with Boston today—Cabot, Lowell, Jackson, Higginson, Peabody, Gardner, and the like—are those of Essex County families who moved to Boston after the Revolution to fill the places left vacant by the Loyalist migration.

The Revolution completely altered the pattern of trade, for at its close, so far as the Empire was concerned, Boston merchants were no longer colonists; they had automatically become foreigners. The port's survival in the postwar period depended upon the discovery of wholly new channels of trade. Just as the economic depression of the sixteen forties first sent Bostonians to sea, so the crisis of the seventeen eighties drove their ships to distant and hitherto unfamiliar parts of the world. Samuel Eliot Morison's *The Maritime History of Massachusetts* brilliantly sets forth the development of the China trade, with its ramifications on the Northwest Coast and in the Hawaiian Islands, and the other new routes that solved the post-Revolutionary crisis. This commercial expansion, which raised Boston to greater prosperity than it had hitherto known, was largely the achievement of the new men, so many of whom had moved in from Essex County to fill Loyalist shoes.

Although it never recovered the first place that it had held during the first half of the eighteenth century, Boston began once again to grow in size. With an expanding population, space in the restricted peninsula became scarce. Thus began the series of major changes in the physical appearance of the place that still continues. In *Boston: A Topographical History* I described the process of cutting down the hills to fill the coves that so radically altered the physical lineaments of the place during the nineteenth century.

Fortunately Boston had a remarkable architect to guide the major change. From the seventeen nineties until 1818, when he removed to Washington, Charles Bulfinch was not only personally responsible for the design of most of the new private and public buildings, but as the perennial chairman of the Board of Selectmen, he was the competent head of the town government. To a small seaport with narrow and winding streets of medieval tradition, Bulfinch introduced the crescents and classical symmetries of Bath and the Adelphi. Following the building from his designs of the present State House in 1795 on the southern slope of Beacon Hill, the adjacent upland fields, as well as the streets facing Boston Common, rapidly became a new residential district that bore the mark of his style. In two decades he had radically altered the face of Boston, providing a wholly new setting for the Federalist merchants of the young Republic. Nevertheless, at the end of the eighteenth century, Boston was still, as it always had been, essentially a seaport.

Just as it had been the scene of the earliest political and

military phases of the American Revolution, so Boston had its representatives in the formative years of the national government. Returning from service as the first American minister to Great Britain, John Adams became Washington's vice-president, and succeeded to the presidency himself in 1797. But with the new century, Federalists were overwhelmed by Republicans. After a single term John Adams was involuntarily returned to private life. Although his son John Quincy Adams attained the presidency twenty-four years later, it was again for a single term. One hundred and thirty-two years were to pass before another native Bostonian occupied the White House. It was in other directions than the control of national politics that the city demonstrated the quality of successful continuity.

II

The Second Coming

THROUGH THE FIRST HALF of the nineteenth century, the China trade and other forms of maritime commerce produced substantial fortunes, but as the century progressed others were achieved in mercantile and manufacturing pursuits without recourse to the sea. Francis Cabot Lowell (1775–1817), a Boston importer and exporter, while traveling in England shortly before the War of 1812, closely studied the new textile machinery in use in Lancashire, and on his return home determined to start a cotton mill. With his brother-in-law, Patrick Tracy Jackson (1780–1847) and an inventive genius from Byfield, Paul Moody (1779–1831), Lowell started the Boston Manufacturing Company at Waltham in 1813 with an authorized capital of $400,000. This pioneering plant, in which all the operations of converting raw cotton into woven cloth were combined, represented the expansion of maritime capital into a new field—large scale manufacturing.

In the first flush of manufacturing enthusiasm it was confidently assumed that Boston, while retaining its traditional character as a seaport, would also become an industrial city. Thus Uriah Cotting (c. 1766–1819), the energetic promoter responsible not only for great enlargement and improvement of waterfront wharves and warehouses in Boston but an incorporator of the Boston Manufacturing Company at Waltham, undertook to supply water power for factories. He proposed that a milldam in the Back Bay should harness the tides that flowed from the harbor in and out of the Charles River, a project that aroused vast enthusiasm. Although the dam— following the line of Beacon Street from Charles Street to the present Kenmore Square (then Sewall's Point in Brookline)—was completed in 1821 and provided sluiceways for powering a number of varied factories, it actually accomplished little beyond providing a new and direct road from Boston to Brookline. Aside from a few modest mills, the potential tidal power of Cotting's dam was scarcely used. Cotting died the year it was completed. Boston had no substantial labor force at the time. Moreover, his old associate Patrick Tracy Jackson, who had become the head of the Boston Manufacturing Company after Francis Cabot Lowell's death in 1817, was already looking north for expansion along the Merrimack River, where there was an abundance of power and where farm girls from northern New England could more easily be induced to come to operate the new machines. The advent of railroads in the eighteen thirties not only brought once-distant places miraculously closer to Boston, the lines from Worcester and Providence entering the city on trestles that ran through the basins of the milldam impeded the water flowage and soon turned the Back Bay into a stinking nuisance that could only be remedied by filling the entire area. Thus Cotting's dream of a complex of water-powered factories was realized not by him in Boston's Back Bay but by others in new cities along the Merrimack River in northern Massachusetts and New Hampshire.

In 1820, Patrick Tracy Jackson and his associates, seeking

a site for the expansion of their Waltham operations, chose East Chelmsford upon the Merrimack, where they created a wholly new manufacturing city, named Lowell in honor of the founder of their enterprise. Another new city further down the river was similarly created out of nothing by Boston capital a quarter of a century later. Amos Lawrence, a farmer's boy who came from Groton to Boston in 1807—as many a similar lad had gone to sea—went into the dry-goods business with his younger brother, Abbott Lawrence, and soon reached a state of comfortable affluence as a commission merchant. The firm of A. & A. Lawrence, originally importers of English dry goods, eventually became not only agents for the newly competing local products but active promoters of Massachusetts manufacturing. Thus Abbott Lawrence in 1845 initiated the creation of the new mill city that bears the name of his family. So, although in the first half of the nineteenth century the capital and initiative for much manufacturing came from Boston, the actual factories were at Lowell, Lawrence, and elsewhere rather than in the city itself.

The eighteen twenties, thirties, and forties were years of great change in Boston. By 1822 the traditional form of government in which a Board of Selectmen administered the decisions of a town meeting of inhabitants, held in Faneuil Hall, had become unmanageable. Under the city charter then procured from the legislature, John Phillips became the first mayor of Boston. His successor, Josiah Quincy (1772–1864), undertook municipal improvement on the waterfront that symbolized the growth of the city. In 1742 the Huguenot merchant Peter Faneuil had given the town a market house with hall above in Dock Square that was named after him.

Some sixty years later, when it had become inadequate both for the sale of meat and the accommodation of town meetings, Charles Bulfinch supervised its enlargement to dimensions more than twice the original size. When, within twenty years even the enlarged Faneuil Hall was outgrown, Mayor Quincy filled the wharf area between Faneuil Hall and the harbor, building upon the new land a great granite market, 555 feet long and 50 feet wide, that bears his name, flanked by dignified rows of warehouses in the newly created North and South Market Streets. These buildings designed by Alexander Parris, at once practical and monumental, still provide vivid evidence of the growth of the city in the first quarter of the nineteenth century.

That growth was due not only to maritime commerce and the development of manufacturing, but to the quite unanticipated arrival of immigrants from Europe in steadily increasing hundreds and thousands. This seemingly endless series of waves, which has been described in Oscar Handlin's *Boston's Immigrants*, raised the population of Boston from 33,787 in 1810, to 61,392 in 1830, and 136,881 in 1850. Of the latter number, 35,287 had been born in Ireland. Furthermore, they ended for all time the old British racial homogeneity of the place, which had long outlasted the political divorce of the American Revolution. The new arrivals, bringing with them trades and crafts, though disembarking at Boston rapidly moved west to the expanding frontier where their skills were in demand. But the most numerous, the immigrants from Ireland, having little beyond their unskilled labor to offer, mostly remained in Boston, crowding miserably into any shelter that they could find. As more came, there was less and less space in which to lodge them. For example, the region around Pearl Street and Fort Hill—once the pleasing quarter from which China trade merchants could watch their ships coming into port—lapsed into an overcrowded slum, as did much of the North End.

In the seventeenth century Boston had been envisioned as a Puritan Zion—a city set upon a hill for the eyes of all to see. In the back alley and cellar slums of Fort Hill in the eighteen forties, there was much that no one wished to see and that most tried conveniently to forget. To the Puritan, prosperity in this world's goods was evidence that the Lord had rewarded the right-thinking man. As the town wished to take no unnecessary chances, the selectmen carefully scrutinized all strangers who turned up to be certain that they had probable means of support and were likely to become appropriate citizens of the place. Consider, for example, the entry of May 25, 1670, in the Boston town records: "Whereas Sebastian Batnardo, his wife and two children with Manuell Correro a Portuguesse have been lately brought into this towne from Barbados by Mr. Joseph Grafton senior of Salem and noe securitie given to save the towne from charge by them, they are recommended to the honorable County Court to dispose of them as in their wisdome they shall judge meete."

Such methods could no longer cope with the waves of early nineteenth century immigration. Indeed, no one tried to apply exclusive standards, for down to the middle of the century at least there was the optimistic hope that the white heat of the melting-pot could refine and transmute whatever was poured into it. Thus Ralph Waldo Emerson as late as 1844 could call the United States "the country of the Future," rhapsodize over "a heterogeneous population crowding on all ships from all corners of the world to the great gates of North America," including Boston, "and quickly contributing their private thought to the public opinion, their toll to the treasury, and their vote to the election."

"It seems so easy [he writes] for America to inspire and express the most expansive and humane spirit; new-born, free, healthful, strong, the land of the laborer, of the democrat, of the philanthropist, of the believer, of the saint, she should speak for the human race."

This was the ideal; the actuality was less happy. Hard labor for the men in the construction of railroads and buildings or on wharves, and domestic service for the women— these were initially the only means open to the newcomers to maintain life. Rural starvation in Ireland had been exchanged for urban misery. In 1850, when the population of Boston was 136,881, there was a total working population of 43,567, of which 8,552 were classed as laborers. Seven thousand and seven of this number were natives of Ireland, as were 2,227 of the 3,107 domestic servants. Employment in municipal services was a step up; this eventually provided an entry into local politics, which proved to be the field in which the Irish most congenially and effectively established themselves. Hugh O'Brien, after service as alderman, became the first Irish mayor of Boston, entering upon the first of his four terms of office on January 1, 1885. Although the Irish came chiefly from rural areas, they rapidly mastered the intricacies of urban administration, and in the end all but took it over. Others owned the city; they ran it.

The first half of the nineteenth century brought not only

social, economic, and racial diversity to Boston, but religious as well. This is not to suggest that the Congregational churches of the Colonial period had always resembled doves agreeing in their nests. In 1720, when the Reverend Peter Thacher was being installed as minister of the New North Church, the congregation had reached a state of Christian disharmony in which the opposition stormed into the gallery and expressed their contempt for the proceedings by pissing over the railing onto the heads of those below. Churches were often divided over the techniques of metrical psalmody. In the aftermath of the Great Awakening of the seventeen forties, Old Lights and New Lights reviled one another frequently. But against Calvinism, old or new, which held that God saves men, there began to spread the "new Arminianism" (or as we would know it, Unitarianism)—vigorously opposed by Jonathan Edwards—which held that men helped to save themselves.

By the end of the Revolution many Boston clergymen and their followers found the beliefs of liberal Unitarianism more congenial than those of orthodox Calvinism. The Anglican King's Chapel, left without a clergyman when the Reverend Henry Caner decamped with the British in 1776, was, however, the first formally to embrace Unitarianism. The circumstances were somewhat accidental. Services had been for a time maintained by the young James Freeman, a recent graduate of Harvard College, who in 1783 had been chosen minister of the church, although not yet in Holy Orders. When his application for ordination to Bishop Seabury of Connecticut and Bishop Provoost of New York, the first American Episcopal bishops, met with no success, due to his forthright

22

statement of disbelief in the doctrine of the Trinity, the Wardens and Vestry of King's Chapel, who preferred their minister to the bishops, reverted to the traditional New England Congregational practice and in 1787 ordained him themselves. Thus, a century after its establishment, the first Anglican church in Boston became the first Unitarian church in the town. It was, however, the first quarter of the nineteenth century before Unitarian doctrine produced permanent cleavage and splinter organizations.

The breaking point came in 1805 when the liberal Reverend Henry Ware was appointed Hollis Professor of Divinity in Harvard College. Unitarian doctrine in this post represented the greatest possible threat to orthodox Calvinism, for Harvard College had been founded to train learned ministers for the New England churches, and, for a century and a half, had done a good job of it. The orthodox reacted promptly to the Unitarianization of Harvard by founding the Andover Theological Seminary, which for a time provided vigorous Calvinist opposition. The establishment of Park Street Church in Boston in 1809 was similarly an orthodox reaction to Harvard liberalism. Despite these counter-revolutions, the change achieved in the tenor of New England life, including that of Boston, through Harvard Unitarianism was profound, for as Samuel Eliot Morison observed in his *Three Centuries of Harvard 1636–1936*: "We can never measure the relief, the stimulus, the exhuberant joy, felt in the last century by thousands of young men who, after a stern upbringing in expectation of a hard struggle to escape eternal damnation, entered a college where hot-gospelling was poor form, hell was not mentioned, and venerable preachers treated the students, not as limbs of Satan, but as younger brothers of their Lord and Saviour."

The organization in 1825 of the American Unitarian Association, in which the Reverend William Ellery Channing of the Federal Street Church took the leading part, transformed into a separate denomination what had previously been merely the liberal wing of Congregationalism. The First and Second Churches in Boston are today Unitarian, while the Third (Old South) Church has remained Congregational. This is typical of the cleavage that occurred in many parts of New England. "Channing Unitarianism" came to be the term, as the Reverend Samuel M. Crothers puts it, "for that form of religious liberalism which, while unwavering in its assertion of the right of the human reason as a part of the essential dignity of human nature, still clung fondly to the supernatural element of the Christian tradition."

But even "Channing Unitarianism" proved too confining to Ralph Waldo Emerson (1803–82), who after three years as minister of the Second Church could no longer bring himself to administer the Holy Communion in the traditional symbols of bread and wine. He proposed to omit them, converting the Lord's Supper into a purely spiritual commemorative observance, free of material elements. His congregation disagreed. In 1832 he resigned his pastorate and moved from the Unitarian ministry into the literary expression of the philosophy of transcendentalism.

Although transcendentalism throve best in Concord, or other pure country air, the climate of Unitarian Boston and Harvard proved propitious for literary and historical production, especially when assisted by the proceeds of shipping and commerce. George Ticknor (1791–1871), historian of Spanish literature, William Hickling Prescott (1796–1859), historian of Spain, Mexico, and Peru, John Lothrop Motley (1814–77), historian of the Dutch Republic, Francis Parkman (1823–93), historian of New France and the Oregon Trail, and the poets Henry Wadsworth Longfellow (1807–82), Oliver Wendell Holmes (1809–94), and James Russell Lowell (1819–91) were a remarkably able and varied assembly to have writing at one time in Boston and Cambridge. Ticknor and Motley were the sons of Boston merchants; Parkman, Holmes, and Lowell (like Emerson) were the sons of local clergymen. Prescott's and Longfellow's fathers were lawyers. Ticknor and Longfellow, by extensive "grand tours" as young men, acquired lasting European literary and artistic ties; Motley and Lowell represented the United States abroad as diplomats.

The climate proved equally propitious to liberal high-mindedness in social causes. Then as now, many energetic doers of good seemed more eager to attack the social iniquities of the distant South than those around the corner. Boston was a hot-bed of abolitionist sentiment that could become militant, as on the night of May 26, 1854, when the Reverend Thomas Wentworth Higginson, minister of a Unitarian church in Worcester, helped bash down the doors of the Boston Court House in an attempt to rescue a fugitive slave. In 1856–58, when Kansas was the center of the struggle between slavery and freedom, Amos A. Lawrence, son and business successor of the textile merchant Amos Lawrence, worked so tirelessly to recruit families to settle there and vote for a free state that when Kansas was organized, its capital was named Lawrence in his honor. Although he established

25

Lawrence College in Appleton, Wisconsin, and gave the first endowment to what later became the state university of Kansas, near at home he served as treasurer of Harvard College and the Episcopal Theological School in Cambridge.

Although many Anglicans left Boston for good in 1776 and King's Chapel turned Unitarian in the following decade, Christ Church and Trinity Church continued in the Anglican communion as parishes of the Protestant Episcopal Church in the United States of America, organized after the Revolution. The Reverend Edward Bass, rector of St. Paul's Church, Newburyport, who was elected in 1796 as the first Bishop of Massachusetts, also had responsibility for the churches in Rhode Island and New Hampshire, while his successor, Alexander Viets Griswold, was bishop of an eastern diocese that included all of New England save Connecticut. It was 1842 before the Diocese of Massachusetts had a bishop all its own. The Episcopal church offered congenial ground to certain New Englanders who fled from Calvinism without being able to accept the Unitarian position. Amos A. Lawrence, for example, was confirmed in the Episcopal church in 1842. His son William (1850–1941), who became Bishop of Massachusetts on the death of Phillips Brooks in 1893, devoted to the affairs of the Episcopal church and of Harvard University abilities quite as remarkable as those that the two previous generations of his family had applied to textiles. One might almost regard the episcopate as an occupational hazard in the family, for two of Bishop Lawrence's sons and one of his sons-in-law have also been bishops in Massachusetts.

The most durable of the religious changes of the nineteenth century in Massachusetts came from the growth of the Roman Catholic church. The first permanent Catholic place of worship in Boston dated only from 1788, and until the great wave of immigration there were few to attend it. Its fifth resident priest, a gentle, learned, and untiring refugee from the French Revolution, Jean Louis Anne Magdeleine Lefebvre de Cheverus, who was created the first Bishop of Boston in 1808, inspired the love and admiration of his neighbors of every faith. The ecumenical movement was strikingly foreshadowed in his career, for when in 1799 he undertook to build the Church (later Cathedral) of the Holy Cross in Franklin Street, Unitarians swelled the subscription list and Charles Bulfinch gratuitously furnished the plans. In 1823, Cheverus was called back to France, where he died in 1836 as Cardinal Archbishop of Bordeaux. His long-lived successors—for there have been only five in a hundred and forty years—were all of Irish descent: Benedict J. Fenwick (1825–46), John B. Fitzpatrick (1846–66), John J. Williams (1866–1907), William Henry O'Connell (1907–44), and the present incumbent Richard J. Cushing.

In the decades that followed Bishop Cheverus' departure, churches multiplied as thousands of Catholics arrived from Europe. In 1800 there was one Catholic church in Boston; in 1875, when the see was raised to the dignity of an archdiocese, there were twenty-eight. The going was hard, for most of the new arrivals were grindingly poor. It was made no easier by the bigotry of certain Protestant groups. In 1826, the Presbyterian clergyman Lyman Beecher was brought to Boston as minister of a new church in Hanover Street in the North End, designed to combat Unitarianism by an energetic revivalistic form of Calvinism. Beecher's evangelism extended to such violent anti-Catholicism that one may lay at his door the disgraceful action of an 1837 Boston mob in sacking and burning the Ursuline Convent in Charlestown.

As more and more immigrants arrived, anti-Catholic sentiment grew among some New Englanders whose intellect, ability, and human sympathies were not much above the white Mississippian's who feels that his chief asset is the color of his skin; hence the intolerance of "know-nothingism," which elected a Massachusetts legislature in 1854 that, as Samuel Eliot Morison puts it, "spent its time largely on clownish investigations of Catholic schools and nunneries." In recalling his youth in Lowell, where he was born in 1859, Cardinal O'Connell described the successful effort of the Know-Nothings "to increase and sharpen the bitter antipathy of the native-born Yankee toward the incoming Irish and French from Canada." But he made a clear distinction between "the strait-laced and hostile Puritans and the kindly and intelligent Episcopalians," and exempted Unitarians as well as Episcopalians from the anti-Catholic bigotry that affected Protestant clergymen of the stamp of Lyman Beecher.

In the second third of the nineteenth century, drastic steps were taken to gain more space within the city limits. With floods of immigrants arriving and staying, the population of the city was becoming too great for the confines of the original Shawmut peninsula. Each decennial United States census from 1810 to 1900 showed an increase of not less than 23.6 per cent in the previous decade, while on five occasions the increase was over 40 per cent. The greatest increases were 52.1 per cent for the 1830–40 decade, and 46.6 per cent for 1840–50.

In 1835, Patrick Tracy Jackson bought up the few mansion

houses that stood in large gardens on Cotton (or Pemberton) Hill, the eastern slope of the Trimountain. He demolished the houses and engaged the Wilmington farmer Asa G. Sheldon to cut down the hill by means of 126 oxen, 60 Yankees, and 199 Irishmen, with appropriate picks, shovels, and tip-carts. The hill was trundled down to the shores of the Charles River to create new streets near the terminus of the Boston and Lowell Railroad, while Pemberton Square, with a considerable number of red brick row houses, occupied largely by retired China trade merchants and textile manufacturers, was created on its site. Similar changes occurred in the West End around Bowdoin Square, where spacious gardens were filled with rows of brick Greek Revival houses.

On either side of Washington Street, along the Neck to Roxbury, a new South End was created by filling, with long avenues and pleasant secluded squares. The steady growth of the Catholic church led to important institutional developments in this new region. The imposing granite Jesuit Church of the Immaculate Conception on Harrison Avenue was completed in 1861, while Boston College, administered by the same order, was established in 1863 in an adjacent building. As the Bulfinch Cathedral of the Holy Cross on Franklin Street, built by Bishop Cheverus, was thoroughly outgrown, Bishop Fitzpatrick sold it in 1860 and bought a tract of land near Washington and Waltham streets in the new South End. Here an immense new Gothic cathedral, almost as large as Notre Dame de Paris and bigger than Salisbury or Strasbourg, was begun in 1867 and completed in 1875, at the cost of a million and a half dollars. Although the South End developed rapidly, with the Boston City Hospital, the

Boston Latin School, and other institutions settling there, it was soon eclipsed in fashionable terms by the Back Bay, which began to be turned from water into land in the late eighteen fifties.

Pemberton Hill had been cut down by men with shovels and tipcarts in 1835. A quarter of a century later, the Back Bay was rapidly filled by the use of special railway trains, loaded miles away in Needham gravel pits by the recently invented steam shovel. Thus a handsome new residential district was created to replace the older ones that were being encroached upon by business and by the burgeoning slums. The design of Commonwealth Avenue and the other Back Bay streets reflected the spaciousness of Baron Haussmann's new Paris boulevards just as the new City Hall, built on School Street during the Civil War, mirrored the architectural style of the French Second Empire. But Boston in the second third of the nineteenth century was still a closely knit community in which most things were within easy walking distance of each other. This was inevitable, for people got around either on their own feet or by horse, and only a small part of the population had horses. Dorchester, Roxbury, Brookline, Cambridge, and Charlestown were still separate towns, with lives of their own. In or just beyond them was a ring of spacious country houses, like Shirley Place in Roxbury, the Perkins and Lee houses in Brookline, the Tory Row houses along Brattle Street in Cambridge, Gore Place and the Lyman house in Waltham.

Mass transportation changed all that. The introduction of horse-car lines in the eighteen fifties, later electrified, suddenly made it possible for those who had had to live within walking distance of their work to move out of the city. Like the contents of a champagne bottle that has blown its cork, people sprayed out in every direction. The adjacent towns were inundated. Roxbury, West Roxbury, Dorchester, Brighton, and Charlestown were absorbed into the city government between 1855 and 1873, but everywhere the old line of demarcation between city and country was quickly lost in a chaotic orgy of expansion and not very attractive building.

Down to the Civil War, shipping was still a major consideration in the life of Boston. Just as steam was about to make sail obsolete, the Nova Scotian shipbuilder Donald McKay in his yard at East Boston built great clipper ships that were the fastest and most dramatic of all sailing vessels. But like the choir of Beauvais Cathedral, where French Gothic was straining beyond previous limits of height and delicacy, McKay's *Flying Cloud* was the beginning of the end. These spectacular clippers were fast but costly, steam was about to put an end to sail, and the depredations of a few Confederate raiders put a permanent crimp in the American merchant marine. Shipowners and merchants who had made fortunes began investing them in manufacturing, in railroads, and in the development of the rapidly expanding western frontier. John Murray Forbes (1813–98), for example, after a start in the China trade, on his return from Canton soon became absorbed in the creation and operation of the Michigan Central Railroad and the Chicago, Burlington and Quincy Railroad, as well as becoming a director of the Calumet and Hecla Mining Corporation. Charles Francis Adams II (1835–1915), great-grandson of President John Adams and grandson of the merchant Peter Chardon Brooks (who had made a great fortune through marine insurance), was for a time president of the Union Pacific Railroad; he developed the stockyards in Kansas City, and attempted, with less success, a similar manipulation of real estate in relation to railroads in Lewiston, Idaho.

In the first half of the nineteenth century, State Street was the link between the warehouses of the Long Wharf and the heart of the city, the chief entrance to Boston from the sea. In the second half of the century, the Long Wharf no longer greatly mattered. The name "State Street" had come to denote the financial center of the city, the place from which investors controlled the lines that led into many distant parts of the United States. Banking and investment, with the interplay that they implied with various forms of manufacturing and business, had superceded maritime commerce as the principal occupation of Boston. As will be seen in later chapters, the proceeds of such activity often went to the support of Harvard College or the foundation and nurturing of the institutions that eventually made Boston a center of civilization. The China trade merchants, James and Thomas Handasyd Perkins, for example, greatly aided the Boston Athenaeum in the early decades of the nineteenth century. When John Lowell (1799–1836), son of the textile pioneer Francis Cabot Lowell, died prematurely, his will created the Lowell Institute, which has ever since provided free public lectures of the highest type in all branches of human knowledge. The Boston Symphony Orchestra came straight out of State Street forty-five years later as the individual inspiration and creation of Major Henry Lee Higginson (1834–

1919) of the firm of Lee Higginson and Company, investment bankers.

On a more modest and less imaginative level, there were plenty of self-made men, lately come in from the country, of which Howells' fictional Silas Lapham is the type. Actual examples were the Vermonters Peter Bent Brigham and Robert Breck Brigham, who, having amassed fortunes by grubbing up and spoiling Boston real estate, posthumously redeemed their unlovely lives (in theory) by leaving those fortunes to found the estimable Boston hospitals that bear their names.

E. L. Godkin, editor of the *Nation*, who came to the United States from England in 1856, observed in 1871 that "Boston is the one place in America where wealth and knowledge of how to use it are apt to coincide." The city was, in the last third of the nineteenth century, a solvent and comfortable place, yet with extraordinary intelligence the proceeds of commerce and industry were being used for the irrigation of intellectual fields. Charles William Eliot (1834–1926), grandson of the Boston merchants Samuel Eliot and Theodore Lyman, in 1865 refused the offer of the superintendency of the Merrimack Company's textile mills in Lowell in order to teach chemistry. He became president of Harvard four years later, and in the course of the next forty years transformed a local college into a great university. The creation of the Massachusetts Institute of Technology, of the Museum of Fine Arts and the Boston Symphony Orchestra, the foundation of Radcliffe and Wellesley Colleges for women, of the New England Conservatory of Music are instances of enlightened use of prosperity. There were also less inspired Bostonians who basked in the setting sun of the "golden age" of New England letters and regarded the comfortable status quo with complacency. These were neatly satirized in the anonymous poem "A True Bostonian" that the Boston portrait painter Sarah G. Putnam thought worth copying into her diary on July 15, 1895.

A soul from Earth to Heaven went
To whom the Saint as he drew near
Said "Sir, what claim do you present,
To us to be admitted here?"

In Boston I was born and bred,
And in her schools was educated;
I afterwards at Harvard read,
And was with honours graduated.

In Trinity a pew I owned
Where Brooks is held in such respect;
And the society is known
To be the cream of the select.

In "fair Nahant", a charming spot,
I own a villa, lawn, arcades,
And last, a handsome burial lot
In dead Mount Auburn's hallowed shades.

Saint Peter mused, and shook his head,
Then, as a gentle sight he drew,
"Go back to Boston, friend," he said,
"Heaven isn't good enough for you."

34

III

Unscrambling the Omelet

IN 1800, Boston had been a relatively simple and homogeneous seaport of 24,397 inhabitants of obvious British extraction. A century later, other things than ships were the chief concern of its 560,892 inhabitants, of whom 197,129 were foreign born. Among the latter group there was singular diversity of origin: 70,147 were natives of Ireland, 47,374 of English Canada, 14,995 of Russia, 13,738 of Italy, 13,174 of England, and 10,523 of Germany. There were even greater numbers when one considered the native-born children of immigrants. In fact, nearly half the 1900 Boston population was Irish; when one added to the 70,147 persons actually born in Ireland, 156,650 first-generation children of Irish-born parents, and 19,305 born here with one Irish and one native parent, the total achieved was 246,101. Boston was thus not only a half-Irish city, but the unacknowledged capital of the Maritime Provinces, for it could muster, between actual immigrants and first-generation children, 112,269 residents hailing from English Canada—another fifth of the population.

The 1900 census could unearth in Boston only 68,717 native-born residents of native parents of unknown origin, but as 9,646 of these were Negroes, the number of white Bostonians who might be considered of traditional New England origin seems to have been 59,071—less than 11 per cent of the city's population. Boston had become several different cities in which widely different groups coexisted without intimate relationship or understanding. The Emersonian vision of the melting pot had not come to reality; instead a marked group-consciousness separated newcomers and older inhabitants.

The nineteenth century had seen the transition of Boston business from maritime commerce to textile manufacturing and to the search for capital outlets in railroads and other enterprises far beyond New England. In the early years of the twentieth century the business horizons contracted. While large sums continued to be invested outside of New England, fewer distant companies were controlled from Boston, for the amount of available capital of the city was no longer so significant in the national scene as it had once been. Nevertheless, Boston private trustees continued to show a skill in investment that caused them to be well regarded in other parts of the country, and that eventually led to a wide development of Boston companies administering mutual investment funds.

In these Massachusetts-type open-end trusts, where shareholders receive income proportionate to their holdings from a common diversified investment fund (subject to a small management fee), greater attention is paid to balancing the protection and growth of capital in relation to immediate income than to stock market speculation. Thus the investment of funds in a fiduciary capacity has become one of the most respected professional careers in twentieth century Boston. As many of these private trustees give an extraordinary amount of their skill, thought, and leisure to the disinterested service of cultural and charitable institutions, such organizations benefit extraordinarily from their generosity. Ralph

Waldo Emerson remarked of John Murray Forbes: "How little this man suspects, with his sympathy for men and his respect for lettered and scientific people, that he is not likely, in any company, to meet a man superior to himself." It is no exaggeration to say that the blending of scholars with an endlessly renewable supply of literate and responsible trustees and treasurers has done more than anything else to make Boston a center of civilization.

While the "prudent man," whether in a private trustee's office or an investment company, has survived the vicissitudes of the twentieth century as a Boston asset, textile mills and railroads proved less permanent. The textile industry passed into crisis in the nineteen twenties, and with it the industrial cities created by Boston investment in the previous century. In following years some mills went out of business entirely; others moved south or lost their purely regional identity through mergers. The great mills of Lawrence and Shaw-sheen, for example, are today filled not by textile machinery but by the huge Raytheon or a variety of smaller new industries, while in many of the Boston suburbs—especially along the circumferential Route 128—a bewildering number of elegant new factories, often with cryptically unintelligible names, represent the extension of the scientific imagination of the Massachusetts Institute of Technology and of Harvard University into defense production.

Many of the products manufactured in recent years near Boston are as strange and surprising as the first elephant that Captain Jacob Crowninshield brought to the United States in 1796. Some, destined for the Department of Defense, are shrouded in the cloak of national security; others, like the

37

Polaroid camera, are known to millions of Americans. Its inventor, Edwin H. Land (1909–) is as characteristically symbolic of Boston enterprise in this century as John Murray Forbes was in the last. As a Harvard undergraduate he began to develop means for the polarization of light as an applied science. At the age of twenty-six he organized the Polaroid Corporation in Cambridge, becoming president, chairman of the board, and director of research. During World War II he was engaged in research leading to the development of new missiles and war materials, but in 1947 he invented the camera that delivers a developed and finished photograph immediately after the exposure is made. But even in a technological Boston that moves at the speed of the Land camera, there are recognizable elements of historical continuity, for the chairman of the board and president of the Raytheon Manufacturing Company is Charles Francis Adams (1910–), descendant of the presidents and great-grandson of the Civil War minister to Great Britain whose name he bears.

Between 1800 and 1900 the physical and political aspects of Boston changed as radically as the population and the character of business. In 1900, Bulfinch's State House of a century before still dominated Beacon Hill, although greatly enlarged. State Street was still the financial center, although the neighboring old South End, devastated by a great fire in 1872, had become a retail trade district. The North, West, and new South Ends had slipped into slums, crowded by the foreignborn. A whole new city had sprung up during the nineteenth century to take the place of the older regions.

Photographs taken from the dome of the State House looking west in 1858 and 1900 show very different scenes. In both, one looks over the rooftops of Beacon Hill, which had been turned from open country to a handsome residential district in the decades immediately following 1800. But in the 1858 photograph, the Back Bay is still a bay, traversed only by the milldam and railway lines.

In the 1900 photograph, the Back Bay has become land, filled with avenues of handsome houses whose uniform rooflines are accented by graceful church spires. This new area and the older Beacon Hill are the best residential centers. In the vicinity of Copley Square are congregated the Museum of Fine Arts, the new Boston Public Library, the Harvard Medical School, and the Massachusetts Institute of Technology. The Fenway, designed by Frederick Law Olmsted as an extension of the Back Bay, is attracting many institutions from the center of the city. The Massachusetts Historical Society, the Boston Medical Library, the Boston Symphony Orchestra, the New England Conservatory of Music, and Simmons College are established there. The widow of the younger John Lowell Gardner is building Fenway Court to house as a public museum for the future the collection of works of art that she has assembled in two Beacon Street brownstone houses of the sixties. The Mother Church of Christian Science—the Rome or Mecca of this Boston-founded religion—lies in this direction. Within the next decade it will acquire a Berninesque dome, that for fifty years will dominate the skyline; within the next decade also the Museum of Fine Arts will move to the Fenway as will the Harvard Medical School, with attendant hospitals in its orbit.

In 1909, after forty-five years in the South End, Boston College moved out of the city entirely to a beautiful hilltop in

Chestnut Hill, overlooking the reservoir, that had been Amos A. Lawrence's farm. Cardinal O'Connell, remembering the hills of Rome, encouraged Catholic institutions to build on the hills of Brighton, near Boston College and St. John's Seminary, and in 1927 moved there himself to a new Archbishop's House. In the early twentieth century things were moving west in Boston, as they seem for some mysterious reason to do in many cities.

When they went to the polls, most residents of Beacon Hill and the Back Bay, as well as older New Englanders in other parts of the city, voted the Republican ticket. There were, however, exceptions. John Quincy Adams (1833–94), disgusted with Republican Reconstruction, had become the Massachusetts leader of the Democratic party after the Civil War, while among the older families there had always been a sprinkling of Jeffersonian and Grover Cleveland Democrats. But the Irish half of the population voted Democratic with well-organized unanimity, for their votes were carefully regimented by ward bosses, often the native-born sons of emigrant refugees from the Irish famine.

The greatest of these, Martin Lomasney (1859–1933), whose empire was ruled from a roll-top desk in the Hendricks Club on Green Street in the West End, derived his power from benevolent services to newly arrived immigrants. When his compatriots came off the ship, he found them quarters, jobs, and clothes; attended to their naturalization; and saw to it that they registered as Democrats and voted as he told them to. Thus in an era before Social Security and other public services to the needy, he fulfilled a useful social function. In 1900, when Martin Lomasney was well entrenched in the

West End, John F. Fitzgerald (1863–1950) similarly ruled in the North End, P. J. Kennedy (1858–1929) in East Boston, while the younger James Michael Curley (1874–1958) was coming to the fore in the South End.

Fitzgerald and Curley were to preside as mayor, or to be opposing each other or someone else for that office, for the major part of the half century between Fitzgerald's first campaign in 1905 and Curley's death in 1958. Curley's defeat of Fitzgerald in the bitter 1913 election ended, save for the indestructible Martin Lomasney, the power of the ward bosses. Henceforth there was instead a single city boss, Curley. The political climate of this period is well caught in Francis Russell's recent book *The Great Interlude*; Joseph F. Dinneen's semi-authorized biography of Curley, *The Purple Shamrock*, is a relevant document, while the novels of Edwin O'Connor portray Irish types as skillfully and accurately as John P. Marquand's *The Late George Apley* depicted contemporary residents of the Back Bay. O'Connor's fictional Frank Skeffington in *The Last Hurrah* was to cause Curley, the year before his death, to publish an autobiography entitled *I'd do it again!*.

The election that put Curley in City Hall in 1914 also gave Massachusetts its first Irish governor, David Ignatius Walsh (1872–1947). Although City Hall was a Democratic preserve during most of the twentieth century, the Republican party retained control of the State House for a longer time. Walsh, who eventually went on to the United States Senate, was followed in the governorship by Republicans Samuel W. McCall and Calvin Coolidge. In 1924, in the middle of his second round as mayor of Boston, James M. Curley ran for governor, but was defeated by Alvan T. Fuller. A decade later Curley made it. He held office for two years, but, trying for the United States Senate in 1936, was well trounced by Republican Henry Cabot Lodge, Jr., even though F.D.R. carried Massachusetts and the Democratic candidate, Charles F. Hurley, became governor. Thereafter, the pendulum swung back and forth between parties and between old New Englanders and Irishmen. Leverett Saltonstall, a descendant of the Sir Richard Saltonstall who came to Boston in 1630, defeated Curley for governor in 1938 and won two more terms before moving on to the United States Senate, where he now is. He was succeeded by Maurice J. Tobin, a first-generation American born of Irish parents. Robert F. Bradford, descended from a seventeenth century governor of Plymouth Colony, was followed by the Democrat Paul A. Dever, whose successor was Christian A. Herter, long a Republican member of Congress and more recently Eisenhower's secretary of state.

At this point racial patterns become obscured in relation to party, for the next two governors were of Italian descent: the Democratic lawyer Foster Furcolo (whose name for a time appeared in the *Yale Alumni Directory* as Furcolowe, the spelling he used as a student) and the Republican contractor John A. Volpe. The next governor, Endicott Peabody, who served in 1963-64, although a Democratic follower of President Kennedy, was also a descendant of the Federalist East India merchant, Captain Joseph Peabody of Salem, whose opinions of Thomas Jefferson and his Embargo were highly unfavorable. The Democratic primaries of September, 1964, exhibited a singular example of party disharmony, for Lieutenant Governor Francis X. Bellotti successfully opposed Governor Peabody in a campaign distinguished for uncivil personal attack. Thus voters in November 1964, had a choice between two candidates of Italian descent: the Democratic Bellotti and the Republican Volpe, seeking to return to the office he held in 1961–62.

The results were remarkable in their diversity. Although President Johnson and Senator Edward M. Kennedy carried Massachusetts by pluralities of more than a million votes, the Democratic party lost the two highest offices in the State House. Governor Volpe defeated Bellotti by 23,000 votes and his Republican running mate Elliot L. Richardson was elected lieutenant governor. The most spectacular success of the day was, however, the re-election of the able and respected Negro Attorney General Edward W. Brooke by a plurality of nearly 800,000, which constituted a singular personal tribute to a Republican candidate at a time when the national ticket was being repudiated with extraordinary thoroughness.

The first half of the twentieth century in Boston was a divisive and unhappy period, for, in addition to corruption in local politics, it included two world wars, separated by Prohibition and a depression. After World War I, the pattern of city life rapidly changed. The automobile altered living habits. Domestic service became scarce and expensive, and most Beacon Hill and Back Bay houses required more servants than could either be obtained or afforded. Thus the occupants of more and more of these houses began living the year round in the country. As the children of builders of Back Bay houses died, their grandchildren were apt to sell the properties as unmanageable. The depression, aided by high assessments and the spiraling tax rate of a corrupt municipal government, accelerated the process. The Back Bay looked as it always had, but behind many of its façades were offices, institutions, schools, or—perish the thought—even boarding houses. I first became aware of the subtle change in the region when, leaving my overshoes in a Marlborough Street vestibule on a slushy winter's day, I was admonished to bring them in, lest they be stolen! Beacon Hill houses, which were older and sometimes smaller, continued in more active demand. As the handsomer ones on the south slope became almost unobtainable, the north slope, which had turned slum, began to be reclaimed, to the point where even late nineteenth century tenements were converted into agreeable apartments. An appreciation of the need of preserving the harmonious architectural character of the region led to the creation in 1955 of the Beacon Hill Historic District.

Just as the streetcar had, in the last third of the nineteenth century, caused the inundation of originally separate towns adjacent to Boston, so the automobile, in the years immediately after World War II, turned more and more country towns into commuting suburbs. Middle and lower income families in the late nineteen forties and fifties began to duplicate, in a more modest way, the earlier exodus from the Back Bay. "Ranches," "Capes," and "splits" mushroomed speculatively where there had been market gardens, pastures, and pleasant woods, thus almost instantly eliminating the country that the migrants sought.

The automobile, with its attendant acolytes of traffic engineers and real estate speculators, in the single decade of the nineteen fifties all but accomplished the ruination of both city

44

and country in eastern Massachusetts. A monstrous overhead highway, named in honor of former Mayor John F. Fitzgerald, cut ruthlessly through the center of Boston. The Storrow Drive, which separated the Back Bay from the Charles River Basin by six lanes of fast-moving traffic, hopelessly destroyed a great human amenity. No sooner was the circumferential Route 128—originally conceived to get traffic around the city—completed than the fields through which it passed became the sites of new factories that created urban traffic problems outside the limits of Boston. But these new industrial sites, lying out of reach of the indecent politics and staggering tax rate of the city, rapidly attracted industry. Suburban shopping centers began to siphon off retail trade from Boston as well.

Year by year the city was progressively coming apart at the seams. The initial application of the Housing Act of 1949, designed to provide federal aid in the renewal of run-down cities, only compounded the difficulty. The entire West End of Boston was obliterated by wrecking balls and bulldozers, leaving its nine thousand former residents to crowd themselves into any available quarters they could find elsewhere. Much of this forty-one acre region still resembles a cross between a dump and a battlefield, although four high-rise apartment houses, of the biscuit-box style of architecture and far too expensive for any of the displaced West Enders even to dream of, eventually were built in one corner of it.

This effort of the Boston Redevelopment Authority did not provide a pattern for emulation. It is ironical that while the West End was being destroyed, some of the migrants to developments in what had once been country, finding that they

45

had less privacy there than in a city block, with the added disadvantage of a long commute on crowded highways, began to drift back to Boston. As Beacon Hill property became increasingly scarce and high-priced, there began the spontaneous rehabilitation of several blocks of nineteenth century red brick houses—not necessarily as attractive as those being demolished in the West End—in Bay Village, in back of Park Square. In spite of municipal government and taxes, in spite of the automobile, there still seemed to be people who wanted to live in Boston. Moreover, thanks to changes in the political climate, national and local, Boston began in the nineteen sixties to seem a better and more hopeful place to live in than it had for some decades.

James Michael Curley had been mayor of Boston in 1914–18, 1922–26, and 1930–34. After his term as governor of Massachusetts, or perhaps more accurately, *because* of his term as governor, his luck at the polls seemed to slip. He was defeated for the United States Senate by Henry Cabot Lodge, Jr., in 1936, for the governorship by Leverett Saltonstall in 1938, and for mayor of Boston by Maurice J. Tobin in 1937 and 1940. In 1943–46 he was again back in Congress, where he had first served from 1911 to 1914. While still there he ran once again for mayor in 1945 and this time made it, thirty-one years after his first appearance in the office. His fourth term was unusual in its interruptions, for he spent five months of it as an inmate of the Federal Correctional Institute in Danbury, Connecticut, for using the mails to defraud. President Truman pardoned him after a petition had been circulated on his behalf by Democratic House Leader John W. McCormack, signed (as Curley later put it) by "every political figure of any consequence in Massachusetts," save one. The "glaring exception" was his successor as representative for the eleventh Massachusetts district, Congressman John Fitzgerald Kennedy (1917–63), the grandson of John F. Fitzgerald and P. J. Kennedy.

During Curley's involuntary absence in Danbury, the city clerk, John B. Hynes, had served as acting mayor. When the 1949 election came around, Curley confidently ran. If a stay in jail in 1903 had not prevented his first election as mayor of Boston, why should another in 1947 impede his fifth? Nevertheless, Hynes, whom Curley described as "a little city clerk" and "the Republican candidate from the State Street wrecking crew," polled 137,836 votes to Curley's 126,666, and turned him out. Twice more, in 1951 and 1955, John B. Hynes licked James Michael Curley. When the 1959 election took place, Curley was dead and buried.

The successful candidate of 1959—happily still in office, as he was re-elected for another four-year term in 1963—was the Democratic lawyer, John Frederick Collins (1919–   ). Mayor Collins is a refreshing change from the half-century that preceded him. He has fewer political debts than have been customary. Though he speaks well, it is as a thoughtful, industrious administrator, rather than as a spell-binder, that he approaches his tasks. A measure of his determination is that, like Franklin D. Roosevelt, he sought and holds high office in spite of the crippling effects of infantile paralysis, without ever trading upon this misfortune. In his efforts for the improvement of Boston, he has successfully breached many of the "Berlin walls" between different groups of citizens.

His eagerness to seek the best professional advice is illustrated by his having brought from New Haven, as Development Administrator for the Boston Redevelopment Authority, Edward J. Logue, a man of outstanding competence and energy, who has attacked the multifarious problems of the physical and economic future of the city with imagination and honesty. Avoiding the mistakes of his predecessors in the West End, he has emphasized renewal rather than wholesale demolition and rebuilding. The willingness of financial and business leaders actively to co-operate in current proposals of the Boston Redevelopment Authority is a singular tribute to the integrity and intelligence of its administrator and of its chairman, Monsignor Francis J. Lally, the able and respected editor of *The Pilot*, as well as evidence of confidence in Mayor Collins, who placed them at the helm of the Authority.

The hundred years from 1800 to 1900 showed a fantastic growth in Boston's population from 24,937 to 560,892; in the sixty years since 1900 it has only reached 697,197, with various ups and downs. In the preceding chapter, I noted how each decennial census in the nineteenth century showed an increase of population in the preceding decade that was never less than 23.6 per cent and in 1830–40 achieved the almost Californian "booster's" figure of 52.1 per cent. The twentieth century has been very different. The 1910 census reported 670,585, an increase of only 15.6 per cent in the decade; the 1920 figure was 748,060 (11.6 per cent increase); and the 1930 one showed 781,188 (4.4 per cent increase). In 1940 the number was down to 770,816, a *decrease* of 1.3 per cent. The decade of 1940–50 showed an increase of 4 per cent to 801,444, while from 1950–60 there was a drop of 13 per cent to 697,197.

These figures are for the actual *city* of Boston, without reference to the portion that gravitates toward Boston of the galloping megalopolis, sprawling from Portland, Maine, to Richmond, Virginia. The 1960 census takes account of this uncorseted spread by giving statistics both for the city of Boston and a "Boston Urbanized Area"—horrid thought—that includes portions, once pleasant, of Essex, Middlesex, Norfolk, and Plymouth counties as well as all of Suffolk County, in which the city lies. In this broader area the past decade showed a modest growth as people short-sightedly moved out of the city to destroy what was recently country.

	1950	1960
City of Boston	801,444	697,197
Outside central city	1,432,004	1,716,039
Boston Urbanized Area	2,233,448	2,413,236

Within the city itself, 15.8 per cent of the population were foreign-born and 29.7 per cent born here of foreign or mixed parentage. Of these 317,064 from foreign stock, 74,575 were of Irish birth or descent, 59,025 of Italian, and 55,480 of Canadian (English and French combined). There were 31,971 ascribed to the U.S.S.R., 19,998 to the United Kingdom, 13,047 to Poland, 10,014 to Asiatic countries, and 7,952 to Lithuania. Many of the smaller national groups had grown significantly. A 1900 Roumanian colony of 68 had grown in 1960 to 818 in the city and 2,379 in the Boston Urbanized Area; where there were 281 Greeks in 1900 there are now 5,468 in the city and 18,700 in the larger area.

The variety of countries of origin does much to explain the changes in Boston neighborhoods in the past hundred

49

years. In the middle of the nineteenth century, for example, Irish immigrants had taken over the North End. In the last third of the century the region became the center of the first exclusively Eastern European Jewish community in Boston. Today, the Irish and Jews having largely moved elsewhere, it is a predominantly Italian community. Thus it often happened, late in the last or early in the present century, that a Democratic ward boss, who had built up his empire by assistance to the newcomers, would find that his compatriots had moved away, to be replaced by others of different race and religion. Martin Lomasney, at least, was equal to the challenge, for among the broadsides at the Massachusetts Historical Society is one in Yiddish that he plastered around Ward 8 in 1917 to assist in the election of Charles Pelham Curtis, Jr. (1891–1959), as a delegate to the Massachusetts Constitutional Convention. Thus a State Street lawyer, descended from the Federalist China trade merchant Thomas Handasyd Perkins, was sent to office by Jewish voters in the West End because Martin Lomasney rightly thought him well qualified and had the machinery to put his thought into action.

Many of the national groups that were first on the scene have by now established themselves outside the city limits. The 1960 census takers found 74,575 persons of Irish stock in the city and 180,621 in the Boston Urbanized Area. Similar figures for Italians show 59,025 and 196,883, and for Canadians 55,480 and 246,247. The foreign-born constitute 15.8 per cent of the city's population and only 11.6 per cent of the towns and cities on the urban fringe, making a percentage of 12.8 for the whole Boston Urbanized Area. With native-born residents of foreign or mixed parentage the difference is slighter: 29.7 per cent for the city, 30 for the fringe, and 29.9 for the Boston Urbanized Area.

From a Puritan settlement, Boston has become a predominantly Catholic city. Murray B. Levin and George Blackwood in their recent book, *The Compleat Politician: Political Strategy in Massachusetts*, indicate that the *Roman Catholic Official Directory* for 1960 states that there are 2,560,493 Catholics in Massachusetts (49.7 per cent of the population) and that there were 553,505 members of churches affiliated with the Massachusetts Council of Churches (18 per cent). Allowing for Protestant churches not members of the Council and persons of Protestant background who are not church members, they estimate one quarter (to a possible one third) of the total population of Massachusetts to be Protestant, leaving the remainder to be accounted for by Jews, Orthodox, and the unchurched. The Boston proportion is, however, similar, for, of a 1960 population of 697,197, 334,676 were Catholic, according to figures courteously supplied me by the Archdiocese.

Sir Anthony Wagner once likened English society to "a lofty structure with many shallow steps by which the skillful and persistent might climb, while some others slipped down and many more kept the framework solid by standing still." But, he added, "even those who stood still might find that the ground had moved under them." The same image is applicable to Boston. As Harvard University is the most durable and permanent institution in the vicinity—"Calm rising through change and through storm"—it is always instructive to consider the records of her graduates at different periods.

Harvard class reports sometimes contain the observations of the type of "true Bostonian" satirized in the poem quoted at the end of the last chapter. The sexennial report of the class of 1940 also contained the following entry, which in 1946 seemed less significant than it does today.

> JOHN FITZGERALD KENNEDY: Journalism. Home, Hotel Bellevue, Boston, Mass. I joined the Navy in 1940, served in PT Boats in the Pacific, and was retired in April, 1945, because of injuries. I have had published a book entitled *Why England Slept.* I covered the San Francisco Conference for the *Chicago Herald-American,* and covered the British elections, Ireland and Europe for the International News Service in the summer of 1945. I was assistant to the chairman of the Boston Community Fund Drive, and became chairman of the National Convention of the Veterans of Foreign Wars, for Boston, in September, 1946. I am pessimistic about the future of the country. [Kennedy received the Navy and Marine Corps Medal.—Secretary's note.]

Other Bostonians in drafting Harvard class reports have minimized their accomplishments, failed to mention their medals, and been "pessimistic about the future of the country." Readers of this sexennial report might have been forgiven had they failed to anticipate that in fifteen years their classmate would be President of the United States. It would have seemed extremely unlikely to a Harvard graduate in the eighteen forties that a grandson of an Irish immigrant, arriving penniless from the Potato Famine, would attend Harvard College and become even richer than the textile manufacturers who currently ruled the roost. It would have been unthinkable even with the recent memory of Andrew Jackson, that the great-grandson of such a man would ever become

President of the United States, particularly when there was still an ample crop of Adamses coming along.

Yet the descendants of Irish immigrants fleeing the Potato Famine, given the right combination of education and opportunity, followed the same pattern as the descendants of English immigrants who put the ocean between themselves and the Church of England. It was simply a matter of time rather than of inherent difference. The pattern of the ascent is familiar from the new men who came into Boston from the country after the American Revolution. Many of these families had stayed quietly on farms, generation after generation. Then through education, or prosperity achieved through the seizure of some exceptional circumstance, or better still a combination of both, their place in the scheme of things radically changed.

To take an example, the first Lowell arrived in Newbury, Massachusetts, in 1639. For four generations his descendants lived obscurely, as the early Adamses had in Norfolk County, doing nothing of more than parochial note. In the fifth generation John Lowell (1704–67) went to Harvard College in the class of 1721, the first of the tribe to do so. His only surviving child, another John (1743–1802), who was graduated in 1760, read law, prospered at the Bar, served in the Continental Congress, where he became a warm friend of James Madison, and in 1789 became a federal judge. The "Old Judge," as he was known, married three times. John Lowell (1769–1840), his son by Sarah Higginson, was, like his father, a lawyer and a member of the Harvard Corporation. Francis Cabot Lowell (1775–1817), his son by Susan Cabot, has already been mentioned as the founder of the New England textile industry. The Reverend Charles Lowell (1782–1861), the son of the third wife, Rebecca Russell Tyng, was minister of the West Church in Boston and the father of James Russell Lowell. For generations thereafter, Lowells turn up in a variety of capacities—financial, learned, literary, and artistic.

Patrick Joseph Kennedy, born in East Boston in 1858 of parents who had fled the Potato Famine a decade earlier, began as a longshoreman, becoming by his own efforts the owner of a couple of saloons and a coal business, as well as ward boss of East Boston. He started the Columbia Trust Company in Maverick Square, served in both branches of the state legislature, and enjoyed a reputation for honesty, fairness, and general decency. His son, Joseph P. Kennedy (1888–   ) went to the Boston Latin School and Harvard College in the Class of 1912. In rapid succession he became a state bank examiner, president of the Columbia Trust Company, assistant general manager of the Fore River plant of the Bethlehem Shipbuilding Corporation during World War I, and from 1919 to 1924 was manager of the Boston office of Hayden, Stone and Company. In 1914 he had married a daughter of Mayor John F. Fitzgerald. Moving to New York in the twenties, he had a meteoric career in stock market speculation and in the theatre and movie business, which produced a fortune ample enough even for a family of eight children. Politically he became an adviser and supporter of Franklin D. Roosevelt, which led to his appointment as chairman of the Securities and Exchange Commission, then of the United States Maritime Commission, and in 1937 as Ambassador to the Court of St. James's.

Seven Bostonians had previously represented the United States in England. Three generations of Adamses had done so, almost as family habit. The scholar-politician Edward Everett, the historian John Lothrop Motley, and the poet James Russell Lowell had held the post, but the closest parallel to Joseph P. Kennedy in the series is the self-made textile merchant and manufacturer, Abbott Lawrence, who had gone there as minister eighty-eight years before. Both were natives of Massachusetts who made great fortunes through their own efforts. The chief difference is in their Harvard degrees, for Joseph P. Kennedy earned his as an undergraduate, while Abbott Lawrence, who never saw the inside of any college, only received an honorary LL.D. in 1854. John F. Kennedy, incidentally, received that degree in 1957 while still in the United States Senate.

Other Presidents of the United States than the two Adamses have been intimately tied to Harvard College. At the Tercentenary in 1936, Franklin D. Roosevelt, Class of 1904, sat staunchly in the rain from 10:00 A.M. to 1:00 P.M., declining an umbrella offered him by the eighty-six year old Bishop Lawrence on the ground that "he wanted to encourage the silk hat trade, and to feel as if he were fishing." The Chief Marshal of the 1905 Commencement was President Theodore Roosevelt, Class of 1880. When John F. Kennedy became President, he drew heavily upon the Harvard faculty for close advisers and ambassadors and had the Board of Overseers, of which he had been a member since 1957, meet at the White House. As early as the autumn of 1961 he had been making plans for the library at Harvard that would eventually contain his papers. It was self-evident that in June, 1965, he would fill the role that Theodore Roosevelt had sixty years earlier. This time, however, the Chief Marshal would be not only a graduate whose twenty-fifth reunion happened to fall within a term as President of the United States, but a Bostonian as well.

Instead, on Sunday morning, January 19, 1964, eighteen hundred disconsolate Bostonians gathered in the Cathedral of the Holy Cross, in response to the joint invitation of Richard Cardinal Cushing and Henry B. Cabot and the Trustees of the Boston Symphony Orchestra, for a civic and religious memorial service honoring the memory of the late President. Cardinal Cushing celebrated a solemn pontifical requiem mass. The Boston Symphony Orchestra, conducted by Erich Leinsdorf, assisted by the New England Conservatory of Music Chorus, the Chorus pro Musica, the Harvard Glee Club, the Radcliffe Choral Society, and St. John's Seminary Choir, presented Mozart's Requiem.

From the moment before ten o'clock when the Cardinal went to the west door of the crowded cathedral—on this occasion far too small for those who wished to be present—to escort Mrs. Kennedy to her pew with as great elegance as an eighteenth century prelate might have assisted the Queen of France and with far deeper emotion, to the end when, as the congregation were leaving, the organist brought in the victorious theme of the hymn written after the battle of Agincourt on St. Crispin's day, 1415, this was an occasion unique in the three hundred and thirty-four years of Boston's history. Rabbis, and Protestant and Orthodox clergy mingled with the purple-robed monsignori in the procession in the spirit of Bishop Cheverus and his neighbors of the first quarter of the nineteenth century. The memory of John F. Kennedy had reunited Boston. May it serve to make the remaining years of the twentieth century happier and more fruitful than the earlier ones.

IV

Talking

HAVING SKIPPED through the history of Boston in three chapters in order to show the background that nurtured the institutions which, in Alfred North Whitehead's view, place Boston in the position in the world of learning that Paris occupied in the Middle Ages, it becomes necessary to consider certain of the habits of the city in order to understand how those institutions function.

The Boston temperament is given to understatement and has no passion for change for its own sake. The "booster" is in smaller supply than in most American cities; the few that there are seldom make many converts or greatly influence their neighbors. The treasurer of a Boston institution never emphasizes the fact that the market value of its securities may be several times in excess of their cost. The bigger and better elephant is not necessarily considered attractive; hence, the fact that Boston is not growing is not regarded as a universal misfortune. Nobody wants to see it become a second Los Angeles.

The streets of Boston are conspicuously unsuited for automobile traffic. Therefore, any sensible Bostonian in good health walks, unless the weather is excessively inclement or he be burdened with an unreasonable load. The distances are moderate. Alleys furnish congenial shortcuts. In bad weather anyone with an adequate knowledge of local geography can keep out of the rain for a certain part of his journey by setting a course through banks, markets, office buildings, court houses, and department stores that extend from one street to another. Beacon Street from the State House to King's Chapel, and School Street, which is its continuation in everything save name, constitute a funnel through which anyone coming from the Back Bay or Beacon Hill to state and municipal offices, court houses, and the legal and financial district, is likely to pass.

Thus, if I stand for a few minutes on the doorstep of the Boston Athenaeum at Number 10½, I am likely to see a wide number of acquaintances and have a shrewd idea where most of them are going and why. Hence it is as easy and natural to do business on a Boston sidewalk as it was in the Athenian Agora. What one cannot accomplish there is usually achieved, with equal casualness, over a meal of victuals, generally in a club. There are, of course, some meetings of boards and committees, formally called with due notice, but these very often take place over luncheon. Both the Union Club and the Parker House maintain a large number of private rooms especially for such purposes. Yet the greater part of the business of many institutions takes care of itself through casual encounters on the sidewalk or at a club table. Therefore some consideration of sociable eating places is essential to an understanding of how Boston functions.

Colonial Boston had its share of taverns, graphically named from their hanging signs. After landing on the Long Wharf, the first building that one met on the shore line was the Bunch-of-Grapes Tavern, a source of good punch, much frequented by merchants and masters of vessels, at the corner of King Street and Mackrell Lane. This, like the Green Dragon, favored by Sons of Liberty, the Golden Ball, the Cromwell's Head, the Indian Queen, the Noah's Ark, and the Rose and Crown, has long since vanished. There is no Boston equivalent of the Cheshire Cheese to maintain continuity with the eighteenth century. The name Bell-in-Hand still survives in Devonshire Street, although in a twentieth-century building. "Ye Olde Brattle Tavern" whose recent demolition inspired an outburst of erroneous history in newspapers, claimed to be of eighteenth-century origin, although I was unable to trace its history back of World War I. Certainly anything calling itself "Ye Olde" is presumptively suspect of recent origin.

Eighteenth-century visitors to Boston commented on the social clubs meeting in members' houses. The Marquis de Chastellux thus describes one to which he was taken in 1782: "This assembly is held every Tuesday in rotation, at the houses of the different members who compose it. This was the day for Mr. Russell, an honest merchant, who gave us an excellent reception. The laws of the Club are not strict; only the number of dishes for supper alone has been limited, and there must be only two of meat, for supper is not the meal of the Americans. Vegetables, pies, and especially good wine are not spared. The hour of assembling is after tea, when the company play cards, converse, and read the public papers, and then sit down to table between nine and ten. The supper was as free as if there had been no strangers, songs were given at table, and a Mr. Stewart sang some rather merry ones, with a tolerable good voice."

Brissot de Warville, who was taken to this same club in 1788 and thought highly of it, noted: "Clubs do not now meet any more at the taverns, and this is an improvement; less is drunk, wine costs less, and the whole expense is less."

One such body, the Wednesday Evening Club of 1777 has survived almost unchanged for 188 years. As originally constituted it had sixteen members, equally divided between clergymen, lawyers, physicians, and merchants. Later, a class of "gentlemen at large" was added, eventually to be merged with the merchants to form the present inclusive fourth class of "Merchants, Manufacturers, and Gentlemen of Literature and Leisure." The present membership is thirty, unequally divided between the four classes. The membership list of 1922 stated: "The Club meets every Wednesday evening from the second Wednesday in November to the last Wednesday in April inclusive. By the rules, the member at whose house the Club meets shall be ready to receive the Club at nine o'clock. *Supper shall be at ten o'clock, and may consist of sandwiches, raw oysters, and ice cream or water ice. One hot dish may be added if the host desires."*

Today the Wednesday Evening Club meets only every other Wednesday, but the late hour and the practice of assembling simply to eat, drink, and talk—no nonsense about reading papers or listening to speeches—continues. Thus membership is necessarily confined to residents of Beacon Hill and the Back Bay who have large enough quarters to provide supper for their fellows.

The Thursday Evening Club, which goes back only to 1845, works on a different timetable and pattern. It now dines together only three or four times a year, and someone speaks after dinner, although no clue to his identity appears on the invitation. The mystery is maintained until he rises to his feet. At one time and another there must have been, and may still be, for all I know, a club for every day of the week.

The most widely known is the Saturday Club, founded in 1857, which sprang from the practice of Ralph Waldo Emerson meeting a few friends at the Parker House's mid-day dinner table when he came in town from Concord. References to the Saturday Club constantly appear in the letters and journals of its more articulate members—Emerson, Longfellow, Lowell, Holmes, Hawthorne, Whittier, Motley, Louis Agassiz, James T. Fields. Moreover, three stout volumes of memoirs, often vivid, preserve the systematic record of its membership.

In addition to clubs bearing the names of days of the week, there are others such as the Examiner Club—also of Emerson's founding—the Curtis Club of lawyers, and the like. Then come a goodly number without names, without formal organization, unrecorded save in the affectionate memories of their members. Such a one is the dining club of twelve men to which I have belonged for the past thirteen years. Founded fifty or more years ago by Henry Howe Richards (of the Harvard class of 1898), a master at Groton, it dines six times a year at members' houses or clubs. As original members died, younger recruits were sought so that today ages range from the upper forties to the upper eighties.

When I was asked to join, it consisted of three schoolmasters (two Groton, one St. Paul's), an architect, a physician, an officer of the Boston and Albany Railroad, an executive in a firm concerned with the chemical treatment of wood, a lawyer, an investment banker, the head of a woolen textile mill, and a Harvard professor of landscape architecture. The woodcarver, J. Gregory Wiggins, of Pomfret, Connecticut, was a supernumary honorary member, welcome whenever he could come, but free from the obligation of giving dinners. In my time, the lawyer, banker, textile manufacturer, and landscape architect, all having died, have been replaced by a poet, an Indian archaeologist, the headmaster of Andover, and a Harvard classicist.

The club eats simply and drinks modestly. As its members seldom agree about anything, except a respect for learning and good manners, it furthers no recognizable political, literary, or sociological principles. It thrives simply because a dozen men genuinely like to talk with each other. It does not matter in the least where one sits at table, for every man is equally contented with the chance companions of the moment.

One could no more attempt to number Boston dining clubs than to count the stars in the heavens. They spring up spontaneously out of a love of sociability and conversation. Some, like H. H. Richards', renew themselves over the years. Others, like the bibulous quartet consisting of two members of the Harvard divinity faculty, a Boston trustee, and a Boston wine merchant, who greatly enjoyed dining together and testing their considerable knowledge of vintages, disappear as their members leave the scene.

When Boston clubs acquire permanent premises, they try to keep them as much like private houses as possible. The only places in Boston where one of Peter Arno's well-stuffed "club men" would feel that he had magnificent enough surroundings are the Algonquin Club, built in 1887 by McKim, Mead and White, and the Harvard Club of 1913, both on Commonwealth Avenue. There must be those who love them, for they continue to exist, even though the Harvard Club does so precariously by renting out space to so many other organizations, including the Junior League, that it has rather too public a character for comfort. Otherwise, the older clubs function in remodeled private houses with rooms too modest for Peter Arno's subjects.

The Somerset Club, the oldest one to have premises, derives its name from the fact that on its foundation in 1851 it settled in the granite house of the recently deceased Benjamin W. Crowninshield, Madison's secretary of the Navy, at the corner of Beacon and Somerset Streets. In 1872 it moved to David Sears's singularly handsome granite house at 42 Beacon Street, built in 1819 from the designs of Alexander Parris. Here the scale of the private house prevails; even in the large dining room—added in the garden in 1872—it would be a feat to seat more than a hundred people.

The Union Club, established in 1863 to underline union solidarity and provide a congenial place for those who found the Somerset Club lacking in wartime fervor, has always occupied two private houses in Park Street, earlier belonging to Abbott Lawrence and John Amory Lowell. Thus, President Abbott Lawrence Lowell of Harvard University could reflect that the large club dining room with its fine view of the Common, achieved by rebuilding the top floors of both houses, replaced the maids' rooms of both his grandmothers.

In 1887 the Tavern Club, founded three years earlier, converted small, red-brick houses in Boylston Place into a club

64

house, with the attic modified into a modest hall for plays. By the introduction of bull's-eye glass, dark-oak paneling, and high-backed settles, simple Greek Revival houses were transformed into the *fin-de-siècle* romanticized version of a galiardic tavern. This suited the members so thoroughly that when in December, 1957, the club house was gutted by fire, it was carefully reproduced. When the club settled there, Boylston Place was a quiet residential impasse behind the old Boston Public Library. Sixty years later the library had moved away; garages, nightclubs, and honky-tonks had replaced the quiet neighbors. In most cities the fire would have been covetously seized upon as an excuse for new and glittering quarters. In the Tavern Club, nobody even considered doing anything except rebuilding on the spot. Although some surreptitious improvements were introduced behind stairs, the general effect is as it has always been.

The St. Botolph Club, founded in 1880 and, like the Tavern Club, devoted to arts and letters, happily roosted from 1887 to 1941 in a large brownstone house at 4 Newbury Street. When taxes and repairs became oppressive, it moved to a smaller and tighter private house at 115 Commonwealth Avenue, which serves its purpose admirably.

From 1887 until 1910, the Club of Odd Volumes, a small group of collectors devoted to the encouragement of fine printing, functioned as a dining club, meeting at members' houses, other clubs, or hotels. Then it acquired premises by renting the one story building at 50 Mount Vernon Street, originally built as a stable for a Chestnut Street house. In 1936, when the real estate market was at its lowest, the club bought a large Greek Revival house across the street at number 77 that had, through changes achieved by former owners, become admirably suited for its purposes. Mrs. Henry Whitman had added a music room which lent itself to exhibitions and club suppers. Dr. John C. Phillips, a later owner, had converted the connecting drawing rooms on the second floor into a large library. The club meets one evening a month and lunches every Saturday; otherwise the house may be, and constantly is, used by members for private parties. Thus it has become a center for the meetings of many organizations, a haven for peripatetic dining clubs, and a place where members who have gone into apartments or moved to the country may, for the evening, recover the amenities of a Beacon Hill house.

As the Somerset and Union clubs have pleasant ladies' restaurants, they are of use to both sides of the family. The Somerset Club even offers a few coeducational bedrooms—complete with two brass double beds—for members and their wives. But these ladies' departments have their own entrances, and are, in effect, guarantees of the inviolability of the main body of the club house from feminine invasion. It should be noted that Boston womens' clubs, like the mens', attempt to retain the illusion of the private house. The Chilton Club occupies two brownstone houses on the south side of Commonwealth Avenue, at the corner of Dartmouth Street, while the Women's City Club has joined the two magnificent Greek Revival houses at 39 and 40 Beacon Street into a club house. In spite of necessary and unobtrusive additions and changes, both retain the more pleasing aspects of the houses of their respective regions.

With this number of clubs, and with the Boston preference

for keeping a club as much like a private house as possible, the city has never developed a great choice of good restaurants. At one time or another in the present century, people have gone to the Hotel Touraine, to the Vendôme, to the Copley-Plaza (now disguised as the Sheraton-Plaza), or more recently to the Ritz-Carlton for good dishes produced there. The Parker House, although rebuilt in recent times on its traditional site, still produces its eponymous rolls and always offers not only grilled tripe but good local dishes like scrod and cod's tongues and cheeks with pork scrap.

Since 1868 two Jacob Wirths, father and son, have maintained a wholly admirable German restaurant on the ground floor of two red brick houses in Stuart Street. Miraculously it survived the anti-German sentiment of two World Wars and the anti-human Eighteenth Amendment that followed the first. Nothing of importance has changed in ninety-seven years. Some welcome air-conditioning has been introduced, but there is still sawdust on the floor and the dark beer, brewed especially for the restaurant, is the best available. No music, no newsboys, no nonsense; just good food, good beer, and attentive waiters. If one needs to dine in haste, it can be done, but the undergraduate who wishes to peer into the eyes of his girl at leisure, or the man with a book to read or a poem to write, can long keep title to his chair and table, as in a Spanish cafe. Having frequented it for forty-three of its ninety-seven (and of my sixty) years, I have a singular affection for this restaurant and its proprietor. In fact, a group of friends recently joined me in preparing a little volume, entitled *A Seidel for Jake Wirth*, that combines history and affectionate reminiscence.

67

The only other restaurant of comparable age, the Locke-Ober Café in Winter Place—an alley opening off Winter Street with a white-tiled scuttle hole through to Temple Place—rejoices in a men's bar, complete with carved mahogany, mirrors, Sheffield plate, and a bar-room nude. Like Jake Wirth's, it happily and miraculously survived Prohibition. Upstairs are two coeducational dining rooms and a number of small private rooms. The menu is Edwardian in length and complexity; a good meal can be achieved from it, with good wine, either in Winter Place, or in the Back Bay branch, Joseph's, at 270 Dartmouth Street.

It used to be singularly agreeable to eat oysters or clams standing up at a fish stall at the far end of Quincy Market, before going to eat in the tiny lunch room next door. A fishmonger kept opening; one ate until satisfied, tossing the shells in a basket; on conclusion the shells were counted and one paid according to one's greed. The proprietor died; nobody else wanted to bother with this amenity; now the only solution is the venerable bar on the ground floor of the Union Oyster House at 41 Union Street. This brick building of 1714, occupied before the Revolution by Capen's dry-goods store, in which Isaiah Thomas published *The Massachusetts Spy* from 1771 to 1775, claims to have been an oyster house since 1826. The first floor, where the shellfish are opened before one's eyes, is delightful; the upper rooms in Union Street and the branches on Stuart and Canal streets are without charm of setting, although the sea food is just as good.

Nearby in the superb 1826 granite block of North Market Street designed by Alexander Parris as a background for Quincy Market, Durgin-Parke's Market Dining Room used to provide excellent ingredients, simply cooked, for market men and any others who cared to eat well. Now tourists in vast numbers have taken over; the management, catering to their confused search for the picturesque, has installed a "Gas Light Pub," and most Bostonians have regretfully abandoned this once pleasant resource to the tourists, who can spoil anything as fast as a plague of locusts.

The Athens-Olympia Café in Stuart Street, upstairs, next to Jacob Wirth's, provides Greek food served by attentive waiters until late hours, a blessing for night-owls. Only a few blocks away Chinatown offers a considerable variety of restaurants and grocery stores. In recent years Chinese restaurants have been spreading to motor roads. One of the earliest instances of this suburbanization opened on Route 28 in North Reading with a sign advertising "CHINESE COOKING—BOSTON STYLE." The *New Yorker* and others laughed so much over this that the sign was altered to "ALL CHINESE DELECTABLE DELICACIES" and thus we lost the proof that there is a "Boston style," even in Chinese cooking.

The sources of good raw materials furnish congenial meeting places. The butcher stalls of Faneuil Hall and Quincy Market still provide admirable meat, free from the contamination of cellophane. Sanborn's fish market, although pushed out of its quarters in Dock Square by demolition for the new City Hall, has settled in a granite building in Merchants Row and looks as if it had always been there. An architect engaged in remodeling indiscreetly put in fluorescent lights, which made the freshest fish look so anaemic that the management promptly ripped them out. Cheney's drugstore nearby, although it has regrettably modernized its decor, can still supply saffron, Bulgarian attar of roses, and almost any conceivable herb or spice. By following a labyrinthine footpath under the John F. Fitzgerald Expressway, one is in the North End, where Italian grocers and butchers offer oil, *pasta,* cheese, octopus, artichokes, and calf's brains.

Heading in the other direction, toward the South Cove, one finds not only Chinese but Greek grocers. These are small and individualistic establishments in contrast to the authorized version of Boston grocers, the S. S. Pierce Company, in business since 1831, whose admirable products can be had not only in ten stores of their own, but through distributors in thirty-eight of the fifty states as well as in the District of Columbia, the Virgin Islands, Montreal, Toronto, and even at Fortnum & Mason in London. S. S. Pierce's Tremont Street shop, facing the Common, and the Summer Street combination of Berenson's Liquor Mart with the older firm of Charles L. Richardson and Company, offer a sufficient choice of thoughtfully-imported wines and spirits to keep even members of André L. Simon's Wine and Food Society— of which there is a flourishing Boston branch—happy. All these are places where a man is likely to meet his friends.

It goes without saying that in a city where people like to dine at home or in clubs converted from private houses, there are no traditional balls or large public events of long standing. Now and then, stationers, hotel keepers, and musicians try to invent substitutes, just as florists have concocted Mothers' Day, and retail stores have turned Christmas into a commercial Saturnalia beginning not later than Thanksgiving. But large public gatherings of any sort have little appeal, for most Bostonians abominate publicity, give an almost clandestine quality to their good works, and hate being in a crowd. They naturally gravitate toward more specialized gatherings of people of mutual interests. This tendency, like the previously noted presence of good trustees and treasurers, has had much to do with the development of the institutions described in the following chapters.

V

Thinking

THE AMERICAN ACADEMY OF ARTS AND SCIENCES, the second oldest learned society in the United States, counts John Adams, the second President of the United States, not only as its second president but as its founder. His inspiration admittedly started with the American Philosophical Society, which he came to know while in Philadelphia as a delegate to the Continental Congress. On a hot August Sunday morning in 1776, John Adams attended a Baptist meeting in Philadelphia and was disgusted by the furious vociferating boisterousness of the preacher. In writing home to his wife he compared "scholars educated at the southward" and "southern preachers" unfavorably with products of Harvard College: "Particular gentlemen here, who have improved upon their situation by travel, shine; but in general, old Massachusetts outshines her younger sisters. Still in several particulars they have more wit than we. They have societies, the Philosophical Society particularly, which excites a scientific emulation, and propagates their fame. If ever I get through this scene of politics and war, I will spend the remainder of my days in endeavoring to instruct my countrymen in the art of making the most of their abilities and virtues; an art which they have hitherto too much neglected. A philosophical society shall be established at Boston, if I have wit and address enough to accomplish it, sometime or other."

In the Continental Congress he had introduced a resolution that each colony establish a "society for the encouragement of agriculture, arts, manufactures, and commerce" and "maintain a correspondence between such societies, that the rich and natural advantages of this country, for supporting its inhabitants, may not be neglected."

Such thoughts were constantly in John Adams' mind. Recalling the events leading to the foundation of the Academy in 1780, he wrote in 1809: "When I was in Europe, in the years 1778 and 1779, in the commission to the King of France, with Dr. Franklin and Mr. Arthur Lee, I had opportunities to see the king's collection and many others, which increased my wishes that nature might be examined and studied in my own country, as it was in others.

"In France, among the academicians and other men of science and letters, I was frequently entertained with inquiries concerning the Philosophical Society of Philadelphia, and with eulogiums on the wisdom of that institution, and enconiums on some publications in their transactions. These conversations suggested to me the idea of such an establishment at Boston, where I knew there was as much love of science, and as many gentlemen who were capable of pursuing it, as in any other city of its size.

"In 1779, I returned to Boston in the French frigate *Le Sensible*, with the Chevalier de la Luzerne and M. Marbois. The corporation of Harvard College gave a public dinner in honor of the French ambassador and his suite, and did me the honor of an invitation to dine with them. At table, in the Philosophy Chamber, I chanced to sit next to Dr. Cooper [Rev. Samuel Cooper, Fellow of Harvard College, 1767–83]. I entertained him during the whole of the time we were together, with an account of Arnold's collections [of natural history at Norwalk, Connecticut], the collections I had seen in Europe, the compliments I had heard in France upon the Philosophical Society at Philadelphia, and concluded with proposing that the future legislature of Massachusetts should constitute an academy of arts and sciences.

"The doctor at first hesitated, thought it would be difficult to find members who would attend to it; but his principal objection was, that it would injure Harvard College, by setting up a rival to it that might draw the attention and affections of the public in some degree from it. To this I answered,—first, that there were certainly men of learning enough that might compose a society sufficiently numerous; and secondly, that instead of being a rival to the university, it would be an honor and advantage to it. That the president and principal professors would no doubt be always members of it; and the meetings might be ordered, wholly or in part, at the college and in that room. The doctor at length appeared better satisfied; and I entreated him to propagate the idea and the plan, as far and as soon as his discretion would justify. The doctor accordingly did diffuse the project so judiciously and effectively, that the first legislature under the new constitution adopted and established it by law.

"Afterwards, when attending the convention for framing the constitution, I mentioned the subject to several of the

74

members, and when I was appointed to the subcommittee to make a draught of a project for a constitution, my mind and heart were so full of this subject, that I inserted the chapter fifth, section second."

This section, concerning the encouragement of learning, was a characteristic and unique contribution of John Adams to the constitution of Massachusetts. As his grandson, Charles Francis Adams, observed some seventy years later: "The recognition of the obligation of the state to promote a higher and more extended policy than is embraced in the protection of the temporal interests and political rights of the individual, however understood among enlightened minds, had not at that time been formally made a part of the organic law." After indicating that "it shall be the duty of legislators and magistrates, in all future periods, to cherish the interests of literature and the sciences, and all seminaries of them," and enumerating Harvard University and public and grammer schools, John Adams continued: ". . . to encourage private societies and public institutions, rewards and immunities, for the promotion of agriculture, arts, sciences, commerce, trades, manufactures, and a natural history of the country; to coun-tenance and inculcate the principles of humanity and general benevolence, public and private charity, industry and frugal-ity, honesty and punctuality in their dealings; sincerity, good humor, and all social affections, and generous sentiments among the people."

John Adams confessed, in his 1809 memorandum, that he was "somewhat apprehensive that criticism and objections would be made to the section, and particularly that the 'natural history,' and the 'good humor' would be stricken out; but the whole was received very kindly, and passed the convention unanimously, without amendment."

Four months after his return from France, John Adams was off to Europe once more on a diplomatic mission. He sailed on November 13, 1779, again in *Le Sensible*, and was abroad in France, the Netherlands, and England until the spring of 1788. In his absence the Reverend Samuel Cooper indeed acted "judiciously and effectively" upon the subject that John Adams had broached at the Harvard Corporation dinner on August 24, 1779. "An Act to incorporate a Society for the cultivation and promotion of Arts and Sciences" was read for the first time in the Massachusetts House of Representatives on December 15, 1779, and was passed on May 4, 1780. In accordance with this act a charter was granted incorporating Adams, Cooper, and sixty other citizens of Massachusetts into "a Body Politic and Corporate, by the name of the American Academy of Arts and Sciences." The charter thus defined the "end and design" of the Academy: ". . . to promote and encourage the knowledge of the antiquities of America, and of the natural history of the country, and to determine the uses to which the various natural productions of the country may be applied; to promote and encourage medical discoveries, mathematical disquisitions, philosophical inquiries and experiments; astronomical, meteorological, and geographical observations, and improvements in agriculture, arts, manufactures, and commerce; and in fine, to cultivate every art and science which may tend to advance the interest, honor, dignity, and happiness of a free, independent, and virtuous people."

The final paragraph of the charter provided "that the place where the first meeting of the Fellows of the said Academy shall be held, shall be the Philosophy Chamber in the University of Cambridge; and that the Honorable James Bowdoin, Esq., be, and hereby is, authorized and empowered to fix the time of the said meeting."

Hardly had this meeting taken place before John Adams was spreading the word in Europe of the Academy's foundation. On August 22, 1780, he sent Jean Luzac, publisher of *Nouvelles extraordinaires de divers endroits*, popularly known as the *Gazette de Leyde*, copies of the Academy's charter and recent publications of the American Philosophical Society, explaining in his covering letter: "At a time when the English Emissaries are filling all Europe with their confident assertions, of the distress of the Americans, the inclosed Papers show that both at Philadelphia and Boston, the People are so much at their Ease, as to be busily employed in the pursuits of the Arts of Peace." Luzac achieved something of an eighteenth-century "scoop" by publishing a French translation of the Academy's charter, with a paraphrase of John Adams' letter, in the August 29, 1780, issue of his *Gazette*, one day previous to the third meeting of the Academy, at which statutes were adopted and Governor Bowdoin was elected president and Samuel Cooper vice-president.

For the next sixty years the Academy convened quarterly, with a reasonable pattern of summer and autumn meetings at Harvard College and winter and spring meetings at a variety of places in Boston. When Bowdoin was formally inducted at the fourth meeting on November 8, 1780, he gave a "philosophical discourse" that was soon printed in pamphlet form and subsequently included as the leading article in the first volume of the Academy's *Memoirs*. A fortnight before this affirmation of faith in the experimental principle, the Academy and the University had already sent a scientific expedition to Penobscot Bay to observe a total eclipse of the sun. Samuel Williams, Hollis professor of mathematics and natural philosophy and a member of the Council of the Academy, was the leader. The party included Stephen Sewall, Hancock Professor of Hebrew and vice-treasurer of the Academy, John Winthrop, librarian of the University and cabinet keeper of the Academy, Fortesque Vernon, who had taken his A.B. degree at the last Commencement, and six undergraduates. The Commonwealth, "though involved in all the calamities and distresses of a severe war . . . discovered all the attention and readiness to promote the cause of science" by providing transportation in the State galley *Lincoln*.

The party embarked on October 9, 1780. The officer in command of the British garrison permitted the expedition to enter the enemy-hold Penobscot Bay, while Captain Henry Mowatt of HMS *Albany* made himself most helpful. Landing at Islesboro on the 19th, the party set up their instruments. There were two days of thick fog, and when the eclipse took place on the 27th, the observers found to their sorrow that they were just outside the path of totality. With the limited time allowed for this excursion into enemy-held territory, they had not had sufficient opportunity to check their latitude. By the curious workings of what Horace Walpole called serendipity—"the faculty of making happy and unexpected discoveries by accident"—their location made them the first to see and record what are now known to astronomers as

"Bailey's Beads." Fifty years later, Bailey in England gave his name to the effect of beads of light along the edge of the sun, a few seconds before or after totality, that result from the almost completely obscured sun shining through the mountain-lined valleys of the moon. This phenomenon was, however, first described by the new academicians from Cambridge, looking through their telescopes in Isleboro, as a result of the respect for learning shown alike by neighbor and enemy during the American Revolution. The results of this and numerous other experiments were published in 1785 in a handsome 622-page illustrated quarto volume of *Memoirs*.

James Bowdoin held the presidency of the Academy until his death on November 6, 1790. The following spring John Adams, then Vice-President of the United States, was elected to succeed him. While two generations of Adamses have been Presidents of the United States, three have presided over the American Academy of Arts and Sciences. John Adams was president of the Academy from 1791 to 1814; his son, John Quincy Adams, and his grandson, Charles Francis Adams, have held the same office, while his great-great-grandson, Thomas Boylston Adams, has been the Academy's treasurer since 1955.

A decade after the founding of the American Academy of Arts and Sciences, the Reverend Jeremy Belknap (1744–98), minister of the Federal Street Church in Boston, met with a small group of like-minded friends to consider the formation of "an Antiquarian Society" whose purpose would be "collecting, preserving and communicating the Antiquities of America." Thus on January 24, 1791, was organized the Massachusetts Historical Society, the first body in the United States to be concerned with American history. Dr. Belknap's group of ten men—clergymen, lawyers, merchants, and public figures—began work decades before colleges concerned themselves with formal instruction in American history, and ninety-three years prior to the founding of the American Historical Association.

The new society's energetic theory of collecting was summarized in a letter, often subsequently quoted, of February 19, 1791, in which Dr. Belknap wrote to Ebenezer Hazard, who was to be the first corresponding member: "We intend to be an *active*, not a *passive*, literary body; not to lie waiting, like a bed of oysters, for the tide (of communication) to flow in upon us, but to *seek* and *find*, to *preserve* and *communicate*, literary intelligence, especially in the historical way." And again in 1795, when he was about to seek the papers of John Hancock and Samuel Adams, Belknap again wrote Hazard: "There is nothing like having a *good repository*, and keeping a *good lookout*, not waiting at home for things to fall into the lap, but prowling about like a wolf for the prey."

The unswerving pursuit of these principles over nearly a century and three quarters has brought the Massachusetts Historical Society one of the great manuscript collections in American history, and has, by way of "communication" resulted in the publication of seventy-nine volumes of *Collections*, seventy-four volumes of its *Proceedings*, as well as close to a hundred titles outside these numbered series.

More will be said of the Massachusetts Historical Society later in this chapter. What must be noted here is that Dr. Belknap's initial proposal of 1790 for its organization included the provision that its "quarterly meetings shall be held on the days next following those appointed for the meetings of the American Academy of Arts and Sciences." The pattern persists today, although both organizations now meet monthly from October to May. The Academy meets on second Wednesday evenings, the Society on second Thursday afternoons. A small number of gentlemen still follow each other about in this way. Thomas Boylston Adams, treasurer of the Academy, is simultaneously president of the Massachusetts Historical Society. In addition to being recording secretary of the Society, I am librarian of the Academy, as the first librarian of the Boston Athenaeum, William Smith Shaw, was from 1818 to 1823. Such coincidences are neither wholly accidental nor consciously arrived at. In the first place, the Boston temperament more readily accepts change in large matters than in small ones, and in ideas rather than in the details of daily life. If people do not tinker endlessly with dates and times of meetings, one knows, without recourse to notices or engagement books, when certain things occur, thus avoiding conflicts and minor hassles. In the second place, Boston institutions are usually on good terms with each other, with remarkably little duplication, empire-building, or internecine warfare. It is recognized that, as there is only so much time and money available, it is undesirable to waste either. In the third place, a respect for learning, reaching back to Puritan beginnings, caused the development of a tradition of non-academic scholarship in which professionals and amateurs happily foregather both in the older learned societies and the multiplicity of clubs. Thus Bostonians of many sorts are constantly doing business with each other—and sometimes with themselves in different capacities—in a great variety of places.

The latter tendency is reflected in the housing of the American Academy of Arts and Sciences during the nineteenth century. In 1817 it settled in with the Boston Athenaeum, then in a house on Tremont Street overlooking the King's Chapel burying ground. Five years later, when the Athenaeum moved to new quarters on Pearl Street, the Academy went along. By 1829 the new Athenaeum building was becoming overcrowded. In the election of 1828, John Quincy Adams, president of the Academy since 1820, nominated for a second term as President of the United States, had been defeated by Andrew Jackson. When Adams returned home in June, 1829, with the expectation of passing his remaining years in learned rather than political matters, he met with a chilly reception. His Federalist neighbors, who could nurse a grudge as long and lovingly as anyone outside of Ireland, had never forgiven him for supporting Thomas Jefferson's Embargo twenty-one years earlier. They had, among other evidences of their displeasure, dumped him out of the presidency of the Academy on May 26, 1829, electing to his place the upright, tight-lipped, and vinegary navigator, Nathaniel Bowditch.

Bowditch, who was then actuary of the Massachusetts Hospital Life Insurance Company, moved the Academy to the 50 State Street premises of that firm. Such an association seemed entirely reasonable to Bostonians of the period, particularly as the company's charter of 1818 obligated it to pay one-third of the net profits of its life insurance business to the support of the Massachusetts General Hospital. In a similar example of the combination of business and learning, the Massachusetts Historical Society and the Provident Institution for Savings from 1833 to 1856 shared a building at 30 Tremont Street, on the site where the Athenaeum had been until 1822. Here James Savage, an officer of both organizations, would run happily up and down stairs as he turned from receiving deposits to editing historical documents. After Bowditch's death in 1838, which dissolved the reason for lodging with the Hospital Life, the Academy moved for a time to Tremont Row. From 1852 to 1899 it occupied a first floor room in the present Athenaeum at 10½ Beacon Street.

Before the end of the nineteenth century the Academy was again on the move. Libraries perennially burst their seams, and the new Athenaeum that had seemed so commodious in 1852 was bulging by the end of the century. The Massachusetts Historical Society, which had in 1872 lodged temporarily with the Academy in the Athenaeum while pulling down one building and putting up another at 30 Tremont Street, was, a quarter of a century later, moving to new and handsome but highly unfunctional premises at the corner of Boylston Street and the Fenway. To the third floor of this yellow brick edifice, which made up in marble halls and superbly panelled rooms for what it lacked in book stacks, the Academy moved in the autumn of 1899. By 1903 space was becoming short even there, and, after deciding against leasing rooms from the Boston Library Society at 114 Newbury Street, the Academy in 1904 bought property of its own at 28 Newbury Street—a private house built in 1870—thus ending, for a time, its long practice of bedding down with other institutions. The location, less than a block away from the Massachusetts Institute of Technology, offered singular convenience to Fellows attached to that faculty and was no more or less inaccessible to Harvard than earlier sites in Boston.

In 1911 the original building at 28 Newbury Street was demolished to make way for a new one, generously provided by a former president, Alexander Agassiz, and his heirs. During construction the Academy returned to the Massachusetts Historical Society. The new house, occupied in 1912, was a solid and reasonably impressive structure, but lacked the qualities of intimacy and charm that sometimes elude buildings (and women) limited by a determined functionalism. During the forty-three years that it remained the home of the Academy, many Fellows thought of it with affection because of the quality of papers and conversation inspired by the meetings. Harlow Shapley, for example, recalled the occasion in the nineteen twenties when Albert Einstein addressed the Academy: "He was introduced in German, or near German, by President George Foot Moore. The theory of relativity—its equations—amazed us, of course, but Mr. Einstein was amazed, or at least he looked amazed, when his equations would disappear from the blackboard immediately his back was turned. For Professor Julian Coolidge, in a helpful mood, would jump up and erase an equation when it had been once used. Here we believe, apparently, in fresh equations."

Number 28 Newbury Street, however, never readily lent itself to informal use. In addition, its surroundings lost any particular pertinence when the Massachusetts Institute of Technology moved to Cambridge and ceased to be a near neighbor. In 1955, when business had engulfed the region and parking had become an almost insuperable problem, the building was sold. For a couple of years the monthly meetings were held in a variety of institutions in greater Boston until, in the spring of 1957, the Academy's search for permanent quarters was ended by the generous invitation of the Brandegee Charitable Foundation to occupy Faulkner Farm, the former home of the late Mrs. Edward D. Brandegee.

This three-story brick house, on a hillside that extends from Jamaica Plain into Brookline, not far from the Arnold Arboretum, was designed in the eighteen nineties by the late Herbert Browne of the Boston firm of Little and Browne. Its music room, handsomely decorated with tapestries and mirrors, has remarkable acoustics for music and will accommodate an audience of several hundred. There the arts cheerfully embrace any sciences that may come their way. Other public rooms on the ground floor lend themselves with equal grace to more intimate gatherings, while upstairs rooms were easily transformed into offices. The terraced Italian formal gardens surrounding the house—an early work of the landscape architect Charles Platt, which have matured to a mellowness rarely achieved in this country—furnish an ideal setting for outdoor gatherings in spring and summer.

Faulkner Farm has thus provided the Academy with a home that, while easily accessible from the city, is by its seclusion and beauty singularly adapted both to practice of the arts and discussion of the sciences. In late June, 1957, the Academy inaugurated its occupancy with a concert of harpsichord music of the eighteenth and twentieth centuries, amiably provided by the Mason Music Foundation. The 1,400th meeting, held in October, 1957, broke all records for attendance in the history of the Academy, while the 1,401st meeting, at which a panel of Niels Bohr, P. W. Bridgman, Philipp Frank, and J. Robert Oppenheimer discussed "Atoms and Human Knowledge," was again of great size. Now that the novelty has worn off, the average attendance at meetings continues to be higher than ever, even on evenings of snow storms when less widely known scholars than Niels Bohr are offering papers.

The early Fellows of the American Academy of Arts and Sciences were a mingling of statesmen like Franklin, Washington, Jefferson, Hamilton, and Madison, with university professors, artists like Charles Bulfinch and John Trumbull, and men from Brimfield, Sturbridge, Hampton, New Hampshire, and similar places, who clearly stood as the representatives of learning in their countryside. In the nineteenth century, as specialization increased, the rural philosophers became fewer. In the first half of the century one finds such public figures as Daniel Webster, Edward Everett, and Lemuel Shaw, the historians Prescott and Ticknor, the poet Longfellow, artists like Washington Allston, J. J. Audubon, and Horatio Greenough, and scientists of the magnitude of Asa Gray, James Hall, Joseph Henry, and Jeffries Wyman.

The record books and the published *Proceedings* of the Academy follow closely the development of scientific thought and experiment. At the 287th meeting in 1846, Dr. Henry J. Bigelow "gave some account of a new process of inhalation employed by Dr. Morton, of Boston, to produce insensibility to pain during the performance of operations by the dentist and surgeon," thus introducing to the world the marvel of anesthesia. The Academy meetings immediately following the publication of Darwin's *On the Origin of Species* were enlivened by stimulating debate between Louis Agassiz and Asa Gray.

In the second half of the nineteenth century Francis Parkman and Henry Adams succeed Prescott; Emerson, Bryant, and Whittier come to keep Longfellow company, and the earlier scientists have been followed by such figures as James D. Dana, H. A. Newton, Simon Newcomb, George W. Hill, Edward C. Pickering, Josiah Willard Gibbs, T. W. Richards, Samuel P. Langley, Alexander Graham Bell, O. C. Marsh, Joseph Leidy, A. S. Packard, and Charles W. Eliot. Similarly in the early decades of the twentieth century one notes the names of A. A. Michelson, Elihu Thomson, Percival Lowell, Alexander Agassiz, William T. Sedgwick, Maxime Bocher, and Charles P. Steinmetz. Presidents of the Academy in the last forty years have included such scientists as the physicists Theodore Lyman and Edwin H. Land, the astronomer Harlow Shapley, the geologist Kirtley F. Mather, and the biologist Hudson Hoagland.

Fellows of the Academy are elected in four classes: Mathematical and Physical Sciences, Biological Sciences, Social Arts and Sciences, and Humanities. Although their number is now in the vicinity of two thousand, a determined effort is made to avoid compartmenting either meetings or publications according to specialized disciplines. Alfred North Whitehead observed in 1942: "The comprehension of existence requires the combination of Arts and Sciences. In concrete human action, there is always a Science lurking behind

87

an Art, and there is always an Art stimulating a Science. This is the reason why one Academy should include both Arts and Sciences."

Thus this Academy, through publications, conferences, seminars, and study groups, attempts to bring together scholars from the most disparate professional and intellectual preoccupations for the investigation of the problems created by the constantly changing pattern of modern life. Sometimes the going can be pretty rough, but the good will and sincerity of the participants makes the effort seem worth while.

In 1955, with the appearance of Volume 86, Number 1, of its *Proceedings* in a new typographical format, with the added title of *Daedalus*, the Academy made a radical change in its publications policy. There was general agreement that, in view of the many journals of specific disciplines where the results of specialized research would normally be published, it was desirable to attempt a publication of broader appeal. In introducing the first experimental issue in May, 1955, I remarked: "While *Daedalus* does not aim at popularization, it is hoped that its contents will prove of interest to Fellows in all classes of the Academy. Learned writing need be only as dull, portentous, or unintelligible as its authors choose." My successor as editor, the physicist Professor Gerald J. Holton, in expanding *Daedalus* to its present form as a regular quarterly, described it as "a medium through which leading scholars in all fields can address one another" and as "an instrument for focusing our attention again on that which does or should make us members of one community."

With the frank admission that there is little hope of discovering some master plan for fitting our separate preoccupations—scientific and humanistic—into one pattern, he continued: "A synthesis on a large scale is possible neither within the individual person nor among the several fields of learning. But as a consequence the need is greater than ever to recognize how small one's own portion of the world is, to view from one's own narrow platform the search of others with interest and sympathy, and so to re-establish a learned community on the recognition that what binds us together is mainly, and perhaps only, the integrity of our individual concerns."

The concluding paragraphs of J. Robert Oppenheimer's paper in this same winter 1958 issue also helped not only to define the purposes of *Daedalus* but to indicate the continuing usefulness of such an organization as the Academy: "I think that the unity we can seek lies really in two things. One is that knowledge which comes to us at such a terrifyingly, inhumanly rapid rate has some order in it. We are allowed to forget a great deal, as well as to learn. The order is never adequate. The mass of understood things, which cannot be summarized, or wholly ordered, always grows greater; but a great deal does get understood.

"The second is simply this: we can have each other to dinner. We ourselves, and with each other by our converse, can create, not an architecture of global scope, but an immense, intricate network of intimacy, illumination, and understanding. Everything cannot be connected with everything in the world we live in. Everything can be connected with anything."

Gerald Holton skilfully constructed issues of *Daedalus* around such broad themes as Science and the Modern World

View, the Visual Arts Today, Arms Control, Mass Culture and Mass Media, the Future Metropolis, Evolution and Man's Progress, Perspectives on the Novel, and the Woman in America. By 1963, when he passed on the editorship to Stephen R. Graubard, more than twenty thousand copies of each issue were being sold, while virtually all the issues, in expanded form, had become available as hardcover books through commercial publishers. Two years later the circulation had risen to thirty-eight thousand.

Daedalus is but one of the ways through which the Academy attempts to interpret in twentieth-century terms the provisions of its eighteenth-century charter. To me, the Academy is most valuable as the place in Boston where I can most readily accidentally and pleasantly encounter, drink beer, and talk with first-rate astronomers, physicists, biologists, and others who do not normally cross my track. Serendipity is often as great a factor in Academy meetings as it was in the 1780 expedition to Penobscot Bay. Thus John Adams' foundation still staunchly contributes to "sincerity, good humor, and all social affections and generous sentiments."

By contrast with the Academy, the Massachusetts Historical Society has deliberately remained a small body. The original limit of thirty on resident membership was raised to sixty in 1794 and to one hundred in 1857; today it is one hundred and fifty, with allowance for not more than one hundred corresponding and ten honorary members. Although the corresponding membership consists almost entirely of distinguished professional historians in other parts of the country, resident members are chosen from a broader group. Normally about half will be members of university faculties or persons professionally concerned with history; the other half includes lawyers, doctors, clergymen, men in public life, and a considerable number engaged in business or banking. This proportion led President Thomas Boylston Adams to remark at the 1958 annual meeting: "The Society from its inception has been a bridge between the world of commerce and the world of the mind. We have never failed to number among our members prominent historians and men prominent in business life—merchants they used to be called. More than once we have combined the two in one person. This is one of our more important functions. Men come here from both sides of the Charles to civilize and be civilized. Their urbanity is such that they do not fail to help each other. And so our meetings seem each year to be better attended and ever more amusing and instructive."

As there are no dues and no public support of any kind, members are carefully chosen, not only for their historical accomplishments or interests, but with a definite view to what they will contribute to the society in scholarly work, in manuscripts, or in money. Membership brings only the privilege of working or giving, for the society's collections are freely open to any sober, literate, and well-behaved person who wishes to use them. Thus the membership is today, as Dr. Belknap designed it to be in 1791, "an active, not a passive, literary body." On the second Thursday afternoon of each month from October to May, some thirty or forty members, a mixture of professional and amateur historians, gather to hear and discuss a paper, sometimes read by a corresponding member from a distance. The common ground beneath their varied interests is a desire to support and advance one of the great collections of the manuscript sources of American history.

The principles of the founders of the Massachusetts Historical Society have been widely emulated throughout the United States. In my *Independent Historical Societies*, published in 1962, I traced the growth and evolution of such organizations. In some quarters, especially those where public support is involved, historical societies have established museums and developed projects designed to popularize American history for a wide audience. The Massachusetts Historical Society has deliberately chosen to concentrate its efforts on furthering basic research. Thus it devotes itself to the collection and preservation of printed and manuscript sources; to their dissemination by publication, and by making them readily available to scholars who come to the library. The collection constantly grows, for the present director, Stephen T. Riley, follows Dr. Belknap's admonition of "keeping a good lookout, not waiting at home for things to fall into the lap, but prowling about like a wolf for the prey." A visiting scholar, hearing Mr. Riley's report of accessions at any meeting of the society, might well assume that it was for the previous year, rather than for the *month* just passed. Moreover, what Mr. Riley constantly gathers in are not last gleanings, low in nourishment. The simultaneous gifts in the spring of 1956 of the papers of four generations of the Adams family and of Paul Revere was, even after 165 years of collecting, a high point in the society's history.

The publications of the Massachusetts Historical Society, designed primarily for the scholar, are issued as rapidly as modest funds permit, without thought of profit or even recovery of costs. Yet on occasion the mountain has come to Mohammed. The substantial royalties of *The Education of Henry Adams*, first publicly printed in 1918 by Houghton Mifflin Company for the society, have aided the preparation of less widely known but highly useful volumes. For the past decade L. H. Butterfield has been at work on an edition of the Adams papers, to be published by the Belknap Press of Harvard University Press, that will eventually reach nearly one hundred volumes. Mr. Butterfield's brilliant and painstaking editing is designed for all time rather than for the moment. Yet, when the four volumes of the *Diary and Autobiography of John Adams* appeared in the fall of 1961, they received national attention of a sort that seldom is achieved by a scholarly work costing thirty dollars. *Life* undertook advance serialization with dramatic illustrations. President Kennedy—a resident member of the Massachusetts Historical Society and a Fellow of the American Academy of Arts and Sciences—reviewed the publication in the *American Historical Review*. In the fall of 1964, Atheneum in New York issued the unabridged diary in paperback, as it proposes to do with all future volumes of the Adams papers.

For more than thirty years Clifford K. Shipton, the present director of the American Antiquarian Society in Worcester, has been producing for the Massachusetts Historical Society volumes of biographies of Harvard graduates of the eighteenth century, in continuation of the work begun in 1873 by John Langdon Sibley, librarian of Harvard University. Beginning in 1933 with the Class of 1690, where Sibley left off, Mr. Shipton has already, in ten volumes, reached the Class of 1755. They sound dull, but are far from it, for in addition to being a meticulous scholar, Mr. Shipton is blessed with a sense of humor and an entrancing literary style. It is typical of Boston that the director of one organization should be doing for a second something that primarily concerns a third. Shipton's continuation of *Sibley's Harvard Graduates* also symbolizes the relationship that exists between the Massachusetts Historical Society, the oldest in the United States, and the American Antiquarian Society, which was the third to be founded.

In 1804 the New York merchant John Pintard, a friend and ally of Jeremy Belknap's established the New-York Historical Society, while in 1812 the scholar-printer Isaiah Thomas, who had moved his revolutionary newspaper, *The Massachusetts Spy*, from Boston to Worcester in 1775 while Paul Revere was riding to Lexington and Concord, founded the American Antiquarian Society. Although this third organization was based forty miles inland in Worcester, where Thomas lived, to avoid "the ravages of any enemy, to which seaports in particular are so much exposed in time of war," it has from the beginning held a semi-annual meeting in Boston. For a longish period these Boston meetings were in the rooms of the American Academy of Arts and Sciences. Today the society meets at the Club of Odd Volumes in Boston on the third Wednesday of April and at its own building in Worcester on the third Wednesday of October.

Although the scope of the American Antiquarian Society is national, its pattern of organization is similar to the Massachusetts Historical Society. Its two hundred and twenty-five members—again a carefully chosen mixture of professionals and amateurs—pay no dues but devotedly maintain a great library that is open to any qualified scholar, irrespective of membership. During the directorship of Clarence S. Brigham (1877–1963), which began in 1908, the society abandoned many peripheral fields and concentrated all its efforts upon becoming a library of national usefulness within a limited field of American history. Its collection of early American newspapers, reflected in Brigham's *History and Bibliography of American Newspapers, 1690–1820,* now numbers about 22,000 volumes, with nearly a million separate issues shelved in manila envelopes. The society has not only assembled extraordinary holdings of American imprints prior to 1820 but has made them readily available throughout the country by means of *Early American Imprints, 1639–1800,* which is a microprint edition, edited by Mr. Shipton, of every extant book, pamphlet, and broadside printed in what is now the United States from 1639 to the end of the year 1800.

The Colonial Society of Massachusetts—still another small, limited organization of professional and amateur historians— has for over seventy years devoted its resources to the publication of documents and studies concerning the Massachusetts Bay and Plymouth colonies prior to the American Revolution. It has issued forty-two stout volumes containing records of Harvard College and of colonial courts and churches as well as the papers read at its meetings; it also subsidizes the publication of *The New England Quarterly.* From its foundation in 1892 until 1954 it was without premises, meeting at members' houses or clubs, and depositing any manuscripts that came its way in the Massachusetts Historical Society. It too has been a "bridge between the world of commerce and the world of the mind," with a consistent policy of electing young and promising scholars to a company that contains both historians of considerable distinction and Boston gentlemen who may be numbered as well-wishers of history. For instance, Samuel Eliot Morison was elected in 1912 at the age of twenty-five, before he had published anything. The Colonial Society of Massachusetts, by giving first recognition and a first platform to many young historians, has retained their interest and loyalty through life.

After sixty-two years as a peripatetic body, with headquarters only in its editor's hat, the society received from Mrs. Llewellyn Howland in 1954 the gift of a fine Bulfinch house at 87 Mount Vernon Street, together with an endowment fund that would permit its maintenance without strain on the publication funds. Through gifts of members and friends, the house is now handsomely furnished and serves not only as a congenial meeting place for the society but also for various other historical, academic, and learned groups. Among the furnishings are many that belonged to Francis Parkman and William Ellery Channing.

VI

Reading

WHEN CHARLES COFFIN JEWETT, librarian of the Smithsonian Institution, undertook in 1850 the first systematic survey of American libraries, he located 694 throughout the country, with an aggregate of 2,201,632 volumes. None of them were large by European standards. Two hundred and seventy-one libraries contained less than a thousand volumes each, while only five in the entire country reached a total of 50,000 volumes. It is significant that two of these five were in greater Boston—Harvard College (84,200) and the Boston Athenaeum (50,000). The other three were Yale College (50,481), the Library Company of Philadelphia (60,000), and the Library of Congress (50,000). Numerically the resources of Boston libraries exceeded those of any other city, for the fifteen collections within the city proper, plus the Harvard College Library across the river in Cambridge, totalled 198,009, while New York City showed 186,567, Philadelphia, 162,433, and the District of Columbia, 111,573. This is not surprising, for a devotion to books in Boston is as old as the Massachusetts Bay Colony.

When the Reverend John Harvard, a thirty-year-old Master of Arts of Emmanuel College, Cambridge, died at Charlestown, Massachusetts, on September 14, 1638, he willed to the new college, founded by the General Court of Massachusetts two years earlier, half his property and all his library. In gratitude for this, the largest gift yet received, the General Court ordered "that the colledge agreed upon formerly to bee built at Cambridg shall bee called Harvard Colledge." His four hundred volumes were the nucleus of the Harvard College Library. Few of them survive today, for the greater part of the books assembled by the college in its first century and a quarter were destroyed when Old Harvard Hall burned on the night of January 24, 1764. This disaster inspired generous compensatory gifts from Thomas Hollis of London and other friends, and by 1766 a new library, elegantly arranged in ten alcoves, was installed in the upper west chamber of a new Harvard Hall.

"It seems to have been realized then, as today," Samuel Eliot Morison wrote in his *Three Centuries of Harvard*, "that a library is the heart of a university, the first necessity of a society of scholars." During the first quarter of the nineteenth century, George Ticknor, Edward Everett, and Joseph G. Cogswell returned from travel and study in Europe with major additions to the Harvard College Library. By 1850 it was the largest collection in the United States, housed in Gore Hall, built between 1838 and 1841 "of Quincy granite in the Gothic manner, the design being a simplified travesty of King's College Chapel, Cambridge" (as Mr. Morison puts it).

While the Harvard College Library was the inevitable and "first necessity of a society of scholars," the Boston Athenaeum owed its origin to one of the innumerable Boston dining clubs. The Anthology Society, organized in 1804 by a typical Boston mixture of clergymen, lawyers, physicians, merchants, and literary enthusiasts to edit the *Monthly Anthology, a*

Magazine of Polite Literature, met weekly at members' houses for supper, talk, and the discussion of manuscripts. Ten volumes of the *Monthly Anthology* were a creditable product, not to mention the many volumes of the *North American Review*, which owed its foundation and early support to members of the club. The Anthology Society had scarcely been formed when it was proposed to start a library. The Boston Athenaeum, incorporated February 13, 1807, was the result.

The Athenaeum was, and still is, a proprietary library, owned by shareholders but broadly conceived in the public interest. Any barriers that surround it have been high enough to keep out nuisances, but never so rigid as to exclude literate readers with a serious need for its books. Originally its field was universal—the best works of learning, literature and the arts, ancient and modern, regardless of language, that could be procured. In the early nineteenth century this was still an attainable ideal. Under the energetic guidance of its first librarian, William Smith Shaw, a nephew of Mrs. John Adams and private secretary to her husband during his presidency, great strides in collecting were taken during the early years. In the twenties, when the China trade merchant James Perkins had given his great house in Pearl Street to shelter the growing library, an art gallery was added, which exhibited not only the works of living American artists but such examples of European painting and sculpture as could be bought or borrowed.

In 1849 the Athenaeum moved, for the last time, to an Italianate brownstone *palazzo* in Beacon Street, designed by Edward C. Cabot, in the mood of Pall Mall clubs of the period. This handsome new building, combining the functions of library and art museum, provided a sculpture gallery on the first floor, reading room and stacks on the second, and sky-lighted picture galleries on the third. A monumental staircase, which was the result of Charles Sumner having fallen under the spell of Bernini in Rome, united the three different areas, and, incidentally, squandered a sixth of the cubic content of the building. In spite of extensive frontage and monumental facade, the new Boston Athenaeum appeared in the 1849 directory as 10½ Beacon Street. No one has ever discovered why it was designated by a number that would normally apply to two rooms upstairs over a grocery store, but so it has been ever since. The number "10½," modestly painted on the glass panels of swinging leather doors, is the only clue to its identity that the Boston Athenaeum today offers the passer-by. This is part of the general Boston assumption that any one with serious business knows where things are; those who do not should inform themselves by other means than gaping at signs.

The accomplishments of the first forty-three years of private cooperative effort, unaided by state or municipality, were assessed in Charles Coffin Jewett's 1850 survey when he observed that the Boston Athenaeum "is hardly surpassed, either in size or in value, by any other in the country, and its regulations are framed with a design that it shall answer the highest purposes of a public library. Practically it is such."

The parable of the talents—"for unto him that hath shall more be given, and he shall have abundance"—was amply confirmed in the local library scene. In 1850, Boston had two of the five largest libraries in the United States, and a larger number of books than any other city in the country. Yet for nearly a quarter of a century there had been agitation for still more books, which led in 1854 to the opening of the Boston Public Library. This, the first major instance in the United States of a tax-supported library, freely providing books to all classes of citizens, set the pattern for the development of such institutions throughout the country. The resources and the new building of the Boston Athenaeum naturally attracted the projectors of the Boston Public Library. Various unsatisfactory offers of marriage having been made, and rejected, the new institution installed itself in 1858 in a specially-constructed building in Boylston Street, on the site of the present Colonial Theatre.

Charles Coffin Jewett, knowing more about libraries than most men, was induced in that same year to become its superintendent. Upon his death in 1868, Justin Winsor took the helm. The ten years of Winsor's regime were unique in their accomplishments. Like the master of a clipper ship, crowding on sail for a record passage, Winsor in an incredibly short time analyzed the library needs of the city, through the establishment of branches brought books to people and people to books, and secured support for his revolutionary proposals. In writing my *Boston Public Library: A Centennial History*, the most rewarding experience was the knowledge that I gained of the accomplishments of this remarkable man, who transformed what had been a few years earlier only a reasoned hope into the first library of the United States.

Alas for the Boston Public Library, Justin Winsor was subjected to political harrassment by ignorant members of the city government. When John Langdon Sibley retired as librarian of Harvard University in 1877, President Eliot sought Winsor as his successor. The Trustees of the Public Library, fearful of losing him, petitioned the City Council for authority to make a counter-offer of a five-year contract at a salary higher than Harvard's. When the petition was presented, Alderman Hugh O'Brien—the future first Irish mayor of Boston—opposed it. Treating the request as if garbage collecting were under discussion, he protested that the order would create a bad precedent that would soon cause other department heads and superintendents to come looking for raises. Winsor had been educated on the job, Alderman O'Brien alleged, and it was time to give another man a chance. So inexpert a prophet was he that he dared to predict that there were "hundreds of citizens who could fill that place after a few weeks with just as much ability as Mr. Winsor."

Unfortunately, after Winsor's resignation and move to Harvard later in 1877, not a single citizen of comparable ability could be found to replace him. For the next eighteen years, until Herbert Putnam took over, the Boston Public Library slatted about in the doldrums. In this era of self-satisfied and opinionated trustees, the library lost the primacy that Winsor had gained for it. The only permanent accomplishment of the board was the hiring of the New York architects, McKim, Mead, and White, who, between 1887 and 1895, built the present central library in Copley Square.

This great building, in which painting and sculpture were enlisted as handmaidens of architecture, was a nineteenth-century Renaissance palace, built with a minimum regard to practical operation. Ever since it opened in 1895, people have been tinkering with the interior to make it more useable as a library; yet it is, in itself, one of the delights of Boston as well as one of the greatest of nineteenth-century American buildings.

Copley Square, where it stands, was never designed as a square. Like Topsy, "it just growed." The first maps of the Back Bay showed, between Clarendon and Dartmouth streets, the diagonal Huntington Avenue cutting awkwardly into house lots on the south side of Boylston Street and the north side of St. James Avenue, and producing improbable pie-shaped wedges. When the area was still an untidy waste, a persuasive musical promoter, P. S. Gilmore, talked his fellow citizens into building in the region a vast temporary coliseum in which a National Peace Jubilee was held in June, 1869. This temporary building, as monstrous as the music produced in it—the Anvil Chorus from *Il Trovatore*, for example, with an orchestra of one thousand, ten thousand singers, and a hundred firemen beating rhythmically on anvils with sledge hammers—gave way in 1876 to the first building of the Museum of Fine Arts.

In the same decade three downtown churches migrated to the region: the Old South Church to the corner of Boylston and Dartmouth Streets, the Second Church to Boylston Street between Clarendon and Dartmouth, and Trinity Church to the wedge of pie between Clarendon Street, St. James and Huntington avenues. It was 1883 before the triangular lot bounded by Huntington Avenue, Dartmouth and Boylston streets was purchased by the city and named Copley Square, and two years more before the opposite triangle, of Huntington Avenue, Trinity Place, and St. James Avenue, was added to complete the square.

The Massachusetts legislature had in 1880 granted the city of Boston land on the southwesterly corner of Dartmouth and Boylston streets for a new library. By 1887 when, after innumerable and ludicrous false starts, McKim, Mead, and White were fortunately engaged to design the building, the plot had become the western side of the recently designated Copley Square. Charles F. McKim was faced with a fantastic problem in harmonizing his design with neighboring buildings and in creating a unified square out of a job lot of styles. Directly opposite his site towered the stupendous mountainous Romanesque mass of H. H. Richardson's Trinity Church; on the south the red brick and marble-striped Ruskin-Italian museum; on the north the English Gothic Second Church nestling in a block of brownstone houses, while on Dartmouth Street to the north was the Italian Gothic New Old South (complete with campanile) and to the south the ersatz old Nuremberg masses of the S. S. Pierce building. To bring this jumble of dark and colored stone and brick together, to enhance and to be enhanced by the irregular vertical masses of Trinity, McKim reasoned that, to hold its own, his library must be horizontal in emphasis, light in color, simple in outline, and classical in style. So he achieved a rectangular granite building—initially suggested by the Bibliothèque Ste-Geneviève in Paris, but ultimately pure McKim—the rear half of which was devoted to book stacks, surrounding an arcaded courtyard.

A vaulted entrance hall gave upon a noble stairway of yellow-orange Siena marble, with murals by Puvis de Chavannes. This led to a barrel-vaulted reading room 218 feet long, 42 feet wide, and 50 feet high, occupying the entire front

of the second floor, and whose great arched windows determined the character of the façade. On the third floor, opening
out of a sandstone gallery decorated by John Singer Sargent,
were rooms overlooking the courtyard, used for music, fine
arts, and special collections. This was indeed a "palace for the
people," as Dr. Holmes had predicted in a fulsome and
somewhat ridiculous poem read at the laying of the corner-
stone. It not only sheltered books, but simultaneously provided beauty and enhanced human dignity. Mary Antin's
The Promised Land in 1912 contained an eloquent tribute to
the way that this building inspired the imagination and en-
riched the life of a Dover Street Jewish slum dweller.

Forty-seven years ago I began going in every afternoon to
take the taste of the Boston Latin School out of my mouth.
Though I have since acquired a fairly wide acquaintance
with European palaces, I never to this day enter the Boston
Public Library without a thrill of pleasure at the magnitude
and imagination of McKim's conception and the consum-
mate skill with which it was executed. Changes have taken
place. The original Delivery Room, whose oak paneling and
deep red marble led miraculously into Edwin A. Abbey's
frieze of the *Quest of the Holy Grail*, was in my childhood a
dim and mysterious place. Now it is invaded by catalogue
cases, while lighting engineers have dispelled the mystery of
the *Grail*. As McKim intended them, the paintings were
evocative glimmers of gold, red, and white, seen darkly and
dimly; today one sees them, as neither artist nor architect
ever expected, as brilliantly lighted banal magazine covers.
But not even the ingenuity of lighting engineers, the obtru-
sive hand rails demanded by safety codes, or the charging

desks that now mar the entrance can wholly diminish one's pleasure in this great building.

Other changes are substantial improvements. A cheerful open-shelf reading room has been devised on the ground floor out of space originally designed for cataloguers, and in summer readers move to the shady arcades of the courtyard, where, to accompaniment of splashing water, they have the choice of books from shelves in gay pavilion-like tents, recalling those of a Gothic tapestry. The third floor offers constantly changing exhibits from the extensive rare book collections and from the Albert H. Wiggin collection of prints, as well as space for scholars who come for serious work.

Many devoted patrons of the Boston Public Library rely upon its many branches and its bookmobiles, without ever coming to Copley Square, for Justin Winsor's principle of bringing books to the people has been zealously continued. But the great central reference collections, built up over 110 years, offer resources seldom found in other public libraries. In the enthusiasm of the first half century, it was assumed that public libraries would render most others obsolete, and that the great research collections of the future would be in tax-supported institutions. Hence George Ticknor in 1871 bequeathed his magnificent collection of Spanish and Portuguese literature to the Boston Public Library. Two years later the library bought the collection of Thomas P. Barton, rich in Shakespeare folios and quartos, while in the early years of expansive opportunism, many papers and broadsides relating to the early history of Massachusetts, that lay more precisely within the field of the Massachusetts Historical Society, were purchased. Soon after 1900 such collecting was reduced to more reasonable limits, for it was realized that the funds available were required for the expansion of popular rather than scholarly resources. But the fruits of this ecumenical collecting of the period 1854–1904 make the third floor of the Boston Public Library a fascinating place for reasons beyond McKim's architecture and Sargent's paintings.

While Jewett in 1850 reported only five libraries in the United States with more than 50,000 volumes, the number doubled within the next two decades. A survey conducted by Justin Winsor in 1868 showed the Boston Public Library in second place (144,000 volumes, 50,000 pamphlets), the Harvard College Library fourth (118,000 volumes, 100,000 pamphlets), and the Boston Athenaeum fifth (100,000 volumes, 70,000 pamphlets). In 1953 there were nineteen libraries in the country with upwards of a million and a half volumes, in which Harvard University stood second and the Boston Public Library tenth. The Boston Athenaeum had long since ceased to compete with the giants, having narrowed its field and contented itself with a comfortable rate of growth within these limitations. Today Harvard University has some seven million volumes (approximately three million of which are in the Harvard College Library), the Boston Public Library two million, and the Athenaeum only 430,000.

In 1870 the Museum of Fine Arts was incorporated, as an outgrowth of the Athenaeum gallery. For half a dozen years, until its first building in Copley Square was completed, the museum operated in the top floor of 10½ Beacon Street. When it moved, the Athenaeum lent it most of its works of art—including the unfinished Stuart Washington portraits—and converted the whole of 10½ to library use. In 1889 the

Sumner staircase was sacrificed to gain space. By 1900 the building was so overcrowded and in the minds of the forward-looking so old-fashioned, that it was determined to build a new Athenaeum on Arlington Street, where the Ritz-Carleton Hotel now stands. A lively rear-guard action, led by Miss Amy Lowell and Miss Katharine Peabody Loring, defeated this nonsensical scheme, to the discomfiture and continued grumbling of C. F. Adams II and J. Randolph Coolidge, Jr. Between 1913 and 1915 the building was taken apart and put together again in steel and concrete, a fourth and fifth floor were added, and a fireproof and workable building was achieved that miraculously kept all the charm and appearance of the old Athenaeum. Henry Forbes Bigelow, the architect responsible, so skilfully adapted his additions to Edward C. Cabot's design of sixty-five years earlier, that the casual visitor would be hard put to tell where Cabot stopped and Bigelow began.

The present Athenaeum is a convenient, safe, and comfortable place to read and work. It has kept its accumulations of 158 years both in books and in furniture, but (through London and Paris agents) it often has the newest English and French books sooner than its neighbors. It has an automatic elevator and uses gadgets, even fluorescent lights where (but only where) they will do some real good. But the architecture of Cabot-cum-Bigelow, combined with the view of the Granary burying ground, a regiment of marble busts, numerous likenesses of Venus, Daniel Webster, George Washington, China trade merchants and nineteenth-century jurists, give it a character of its own.

David McCord in *About Boston* summed it up better than

I can. "No other Boston institution [he writes] has anything like its antique, endearing, and enduring atmosphere. It combines the best elements of the Bodleian, Monticello, the frigate *Constitution*, a greenhouse, and an old New England sitting room. Some of the staff members have worked there all their lives. The only typewriter you are likely to see is a Hammond, c. 1886, still complete right down to the curved wooden cover. [No longer true; I write too many letters and too many books. W.M.W.] Yet there is on every one of its five delightful floors an unobstructive sense of efficiency gained without noise or speed, punch cards, or placebos. The Athenaeum is a kind of utopia for books: the high-ceiling rooms, the little balconies, alcoves, nooks, and angles all suggest sanctuary, escape, creature comfort. The reader, the scholar, the browser, is king. An anechoic chamber is not more silent. Even the elevator is hallowed, and the prints, pictures, and statuary—from Lafayette to an incredible Little Nell—wear the look of ineffable charm. Accessible shelves and stacks are rich and even great in Colonial and Confederate collections. Here is George Washington's private library; here you will also discover the latest (mark you! the *very* latest) books and that variety of carefully chosen volumes in many fields which makes it possible . . . to dig a considerable distance in almost any historical, literary, or artistic subject before running out of material."

To the testimony of the poet may be added that of the working scholar, for in the acknowledgments that preceded the text of *Adams Family Correspondence* published in 1963, Lyman Butterfield wrote: "In editing the family letters we have drawn on the resources of a great many institutions,

both nearby and at a distance. They would make so formi-
dable a list that they cannot be named here. But a special
word must be said about our almost daily use of the Boston
Athenaeum. That unique institution, from one point of view
a relic and type of an age that has passed out, as we see it, an
indispensible servant of modern scholarship, has not only
substantial holdings of books written and owned by the
Adamses but an almost uncanny number of the books and
pamphlets, in whatever languages, the Adamses allude to in
their letters and diaries. This is perhaps not surprising when
one reflects that the Athenaeum is the product of the same
culture that produced the Adamses themselves and that members of the family have held shares, have read, and have written in the Athenaeum from its founding to the present day.
. . . But what is more than all this, thanks to its vigilant and
courteous staff, both the books and the information one seeks
at the Athenaeum are marvelously and promptly accessible
to the seeker." Mr. Butterfield, after remarking that the
Athenaeum "has, in consequence, been a right hand to the
Adams enterprise," salutes the present staff "together with all
their predecessors, who built, if not better than they knew,
better than others knew."

When William Coolidge Lane, librarian of the Boston
Athenaeum, was in 1897 appointed to the post at Harvard
made vacant by the death of Justin Winsor, he could not have
felt any extraordinary difference in the magnitude of his old
and his new responsibilities. At that time the two libraries
were still of comparable dimensions. The great change occurred in the first two decades of the twentieth century, in

large part through the genius of Archibald Cary Coolidge (1866–1928).

Coolidge, who was the grandson of two Boston East India merchants, Joseph Coolidge, Jr., and John Lowell Gardner, carried the energy and daring of Federalist foreign trade into academic life. Being graduated *summa cum laude* from Harvard College in 1887, he studied in Berlin, Freiburg, and Paris, and did a stint in the diplomatic corps in St. Petersburg, Paris, and Vienna before returning to Harvard to teach history in 1893. Having an intense concern with the gathering of books as the tools of scholarship, he made numerous gifts to the library of collections in fields of European history—such as Slavic, German, Scandinavian, and Ottoman—that had previously been poorly represented. Appointed in 1910 to the new post of director of the University Library, he devoted the greater part of his extraordinary energies for the remaining eighteen years of his life to developing a library that was worthy of a great university faculty.

In 1912 the mother of Harry Elkins Widener, Class of 1907, a promising book collector who had been drowned in the sinking of the *Titanic*, offered to give a library building in memory of her son. Professor Coolidge's organizational abilities were never shown more clearly than during the next three years. Books were moved to temporary quarters in Randall Hall and elsewhere before the end of the year. Gore Hall was promptly demolished, and the Harry Elkins Widener Memorial Library rose on its site between February, 1913, and Commencement Day, 1915. Widener Library, with shelving for a million and half volumes, three hundred reading stalls for students in the stack, and seventy studies for professors, represented the ideal of scholarly convenience and luxury fifty years ago.

In the twenties, when I was an undergraduate, it still represented all that the heart could desire. I had a stack card that gave me the run of thirty miles of shelves. I could read and reserve books at a stall in the stack, and, on occasion, go to the handsome room where George Parker Winship (1871–1952) presided over Harry Widener's own collection. Winship was a curious gnome of a man, lazy and frivolous by severe standards, but with an extraordinary knowledge of books and printing that he conveyed by a kind of osmosis to receptive undergraduates. Great logs blazed in the fireplace under Harry Widener's portrait. There was always a cup of tea, a pile of the latest British book catalogues, lively talk, often illustrated by some of Harry Widener's books or others brought upstairs from the Treasure Room, for while Winship was always concerned with attracting collectors from the outside world, he equally believed in proselytizing from within. He was keenly aware that the undergraduate body contained many actual and potential lovers of books; moreover, in his own offhand and peculiar way, he was an inspired teacher. Several of my contemporaries who have become great collectors owe him as much as I do. Moreover, by some intuition, he quite casually sent me off in February, 1925, to enroll in a course of Professor A. Kingsley Porter's, thus setting me on a path to medieval Spain that absorbed me for the next eleven years.

Although I recall the Widener Library of forty years ago with sentiments similar to those of pilgrims to Rome, Santiago de Compostela, or Mecca, it soon thereafter began to lose its perfection. Once a learned library embarks on a course of comprehensive completeness, such as Professor Coolidge had charted, even thirty miles of shelves get crowded. Thus under Keyes De Witt Metcalf, director from 1937 to 1955, the University Library became, of necessity, not choice, more and more decentralized. The Houghton Library for rare books and the Lamont Library for undergraduates were constructed near Widener; the New England Deposit Library was built across the river on Soldiers Field for the sleeping storage of little-used books not only belonging to Harvard but to other libraries in the Boston area. Thus books once within easy reach in Widener might today be in three other places, not to mention a good number of departmental or museum libraries scattered all over Cambridge.

There are, of course, compensations. There are a great many more books. The Houghton Library, under the direction of the late William A. Jackson (1905–64), with Philip Hofer's incredibly rich Department of Printing and Graphic Arts, has become a treasure house of extraordinary quality that far outshines what George Winship could once offer me in the Widener Room. The Lamont Library leads beginners to their books imaginatively. All eight of the residential houses have their own libraries, as do twenty-five departments.

While what I have just mentioned represents only the Harvard College Library's three million books and pamphlets, there are another four million in other libraries belonging to Harvard University. In the category "Special, Office, and Research Libraries Affiliated with the Faculty of Arts and Sciences" are a bewildering variety. The Harvard–Yenching Institute Library, with 384,292 books and pamphlets, contains more volumes in Chinese and Japanese than the combined holdings in all languages of the five largest libraries in the United States in 1850. Add the quarter million volumes of the Museum of Comparative Zoology to the other specialized libraries in Cambridge; toss in the sixty thousand Byzantine titles at Dumbarton Oaks in Washington, the nine thousand belonging to the Center for Hellenic Studies (on the other side of Rock Creek Park), and the fifty-five thousand of Bernard Berenson's library in Florence, and the situation becomes downright dizzying. In other faculties of the University, the Law School library alone accounts for a million of these, the Baker Library of the Business School for nearly four hundred thousand. And the Schools of Medicine and Public Health, with nearly a third of a million books and pamphlets of their own, recently joined forces with the slightly larger Boston Medical Library in the new Countway Library of Medicine in Boston, dedicated in May, 1965.

Beyond the boundaries of Harvard University there are in Boston a staggering variety of libraries maintained by colleges, learned societies, religious bodies, hospitals, banks, and business firms—close to 150, all told. Where there were five libraries with more than 50,000 volumes in the entire United States in 1850, there are fifteen in that category today within the city limits of Boston. Of this group I have already mentioned the Boston Public Library, the Boston Athenaeum, the Massachusetts Historical Society, and the Boston Medical Library.

The New England Historic Genealogical Society, organized in 1845, has developed a superb library of 180,000 volumes in family and local history that serves the genealogist as admirably as the Massachusetts Historical Society serves the historian. Through the quarterly *New England Historical and Genealogical Register* and a mailing service for books, it reaches members in all parts of the country and serves a national function. Housed for half a century at 9 Ashburton Place in a building halfway between the Massachusetts Archives and the Suffolk County Court House, the society has recently been displaced by the construction of a new state office building. In the autumn of 1964 it moved to new quarters at 101 Newbury Street, which, although at greater distance from the court records, provide more satisfactory lodging for the library.

The Massachusetts State Library, specializing in reference service for the legislature and in public documents and newspaper files, has over eight hundred thousand volumes; the Social Law Library in the Suffolk County Court House, over one hundred and twenty-five thousand; the Massachusetts Division of Library Extension, sixty-four thousand.

Five colleges and universities in the city limits fall within this category: Boston University (521,151), Simmons College (102,500) which, incidentally, conducts a School of Library Science, Northeastern University (100,000), St. John's Seminary (97,500), and Suffolk University (52,193). Parenthetically, one should not forget that the learned Jesuits of Boston College, although they have moved across the city boundaries into Chestnut Hill, possess there a library of over half a million volumes.

The American Congregational Association maintains, next

door to the Athenaeum, the Congregational Library, whose 190,000 books and pamphlets make it the largest of the many denominational reference collections in Boston. Finally, the Museum of Fine Arts offers 115,000 books and 100,000 photographs not only to its curators but to anyone whose interests include the history of art.

Most of these libraries are steadily growing. A few are contemplating new buildings or additions; others are simply sending little-used books to the New England Deposit Library and grumbling about lack of space. For the parable of the talents is as pertinent in Boston now as a century ago: "unto him that hath shall more be given." So it is rare that a person needing a book of almost any description under the sun cannot find it somewhere in the periphery of Boston if he knows enough to look in the right library.

VII

Seeing

WITH LIBRARIES, as with the inn at Bethlehem, there is never enough room. In 1866, less than twenty years after the Boston Athenaeum moved into 10½ Beacon Street, its Standing Committee reported: "As matters now stand, the room for books cannot be increased without encroaching upon the room occupied by the Fine Arts. The household being too large for the house, somebody must migrate, either into a distinct building, located elsewhere, or into an additional building, connected with the present. The Committee believes that if either is to be removed, there would be less objection to the removal of the sculpture and painting than to the removal of the Library. In their opinion the time has come when this removal is essential to the interest of both departments—and no other provision for present and prospective wants appear to them effectual."

Harvard College had no means of exhibiting a fine collection of three thousand engravings bequeathed by Francis Calley Gray (1790–1856), while the Massachusetts Institute of Technology had insufficient room for its architectural casts. Consequently, representatives of these three institutions joined with other neighbors in petitioning the Massachusetts legislature to charter a new organization specifically devoted to the public exhibition of works of art. Thus the Museum of

Fine Arts was incorporated on February 4, 1870, with a board of trustees that included representatives of the Athenaeum, Harvard, and M.I.T. Although representatives of the city and state sit *ex officiis* as members of the board, the only gift the museum ever received from a public source was the plot of land in Copley Square upon which its first building was placed. Otherwise, the entire support of the institution has come from the remarkable and imaginative generosity of private individuals.

In its early years, while funds were being raised, the museum roosted in the already overcrowded top floor of the Athenaeum. On July 3, 1876, the day before the centennial of Independence, the first wing of the new Museum of Fine Arts—a brick and terra cotta Gothic building of Ruskinian inspiration, designed by Sturgis and Brigham—was opened in Copley Square. The Athenaeum lent most of its works of art to the new institution, thus reducing the household at 10½ Beacon Street Street to books. The Copley Square façade of the museum was completed in 1878, while ten years later two wings with a connecting corridor were added at the rear.

The Athenaeum's half-century of collecting had resulted in the gathering of the works of living American artists and a surprisingly respectable group of European works of art. The Museum of Fine Arts in its first half-century developed oriental, Egyptian, and classical collections of international distinction, largely through the knowledge, enthusiasm, and generosity of a series of inspired and highly varied individuals.

In 1877 the self-educated zoologist, Edward Sylvester Morse (1838–1925), sailed for Japan to dredge for brachiopods. Three weeks after he landed he was engaged by the

Japanese government to establish a department of zoology at the new Imperial University of Tokyo. By the peculiar workings of serendipity this rather tasteless scientist was to attract men about him who caused the Museum of Fine Arts to acquire the greatest collection of Japanese art in the western world. Between dredging for brachiopods, excavating shell heaps, and introducing Darwinian theory and western laboratory techniques, Morse became fascinated by Japanese pottery. As he was a born collector, he rapidly turned to the accumulation of specimens of pottery as a peripheral hobby. Although officially engaged in the westernization of Japan, his keen observation and photographic memory recorded innumerable details of the traditional life and culture of the country. When the Imperial University needed a professor of philosophy, Morse wrote to Charles Eliot Norton for suggestions. Thus Ernest Francisco Fenollosa (1853–1908), the Salem-born son of a Spanish musician, turned up in Tokyo in 1878 to fill the post. After graduating first in the Harvard Class of 1874, Fenollosa had studied philosophy before entering, in January, 1877, the newly founded school at the Museum of Fine Arts.

While Morse returned home after two years to become director of the Peabody Academy of Science (now the Peabody Museum of Salem), a post that he held from 1880 to 1916, Fenollosa remained for many years, embracing both Japanese ways and Buddhism. His interests turned to the art of Japan, which he collected and studied with avidity. Although he continued to teach philosophy for six years, the Japanese government soon found other uses for him, for in 1888 when the Tokyo Fine Arts Academy and the Imperial Museum were opened he was made their manager. Fenollosa eventually found a valued ally in Okakura Kakuzo (1863–1913), author of *The Book of Tea*, who became an outstanding authority on earlier Japanese art as well as a kind of Japanese William Morris in his attempt to blend traditional craftsmanship with the art of his time.

When Morse returned to Salem in the autumn of 1879, he was not only a zoologist but New England's principal source of information about the culture of Japan. A series of Lowell Institute lectures that he gave not only created great excitement about Japan but induced various Bostonians to go there. William Sturgis Bigelow (1850–1926), son and grandson of eminent physicians, had attended Harvard College in the Class of 1871, received an M.D. in 1874 before studying for five years in Paris with Pasteur and Ranvier. On his return to Boston he had little taste for medical practice. Becoming fascinated with Japan he went there with Morse in 1882, where they joined forces with Fenollosa. Being a grandson of the China trade merchant William Sturgis, Dr. Bigelow had not only the leisure to follow his inclinations but the means to collect on a generous scale. Although he stayed in Japan only until 1888, the remainder of his life was devoted to the collecting and study of Japanese art. Like Fenollosa he became a Buddhist, and in 1908 delivered an Ingersoll Lecture at Harvard, subsequently published as *Buddhism and Immortality*. Dr. Bigelow's gifts to the Museum of Fine Arts eventually included some thousands of Japanese and Chinese paintings, as well as Buddhistic wood sculptures, Japanese prints, lacquer, swords, and metal work.

Another graduate of the Harvard Medical School possessed of a China trade fortune, Dr. Charles Goddard Weld (1857–

1911), also fell under the spell of Japan and, through Morse and Fenollosa, became an active collector. Percival Lowell (1855–1916) spent the decade 1883–93 traveling and writing in the Far East, chiefly in Japan. Mr. and Mrs. John Lowell Gardner, who had had Morse lecturing on Japan at their house in 1882, went there the following year. Their nephew John Gardner Coolidge (1863–1936) spent the years 1887–89 in Japan and Korea, although his collecting was rather in the field of Chinese porcelains, now in the Museum of Fine Arts. Henry Adams also came to Japan briefly in 1886, after the death of his wife, with John La Farge, and joined Bigelow and Fenollosa.

During the eighties there were opportunities to collect in Japan that have never existed before or since. As Morse and Fenollosa had been early on the scene and knew the country as few foreigners did, and as Dr. Bigelow and Dr. Weld eagerly seized the opportunities to acquire works of art, the Museum of Fine Arts soon reached a unique position among Western institutions in its holdings of oriental art. A related ethnological collection, uniquely illustrating the life and crafts of the older Japan, was developed at Morse's Peabody Museum of Salem. For the exhibition of this, Dr. Weld gave a new hall in 1907. Throughout the eighties Morse, on saved salary and borrowed money, had been constantly adding to his pottery collection, which in 1890 he sold to the Museum of Fine Arts.

From 1890 to 1897, Fenollosa broke his stay in Japan to be in Boston as curator of the Museum of Fine Arts oriental collection, while Okakura held the post for a few years in the first decade of the twentieth century. During Okakura's curatorship, Kojiro Tomita came from Japan in 1908 as a boy of seventeen to work in the Asiatic Department. In 1963, Mr. Tomita retired from the curatorship to which he had been appointed in 1932. During his fifty-five years in Boston the museum built up many phases of the Asiatic Department, Chinese quite as much as Japanese; indeed, the gifts and bequests inspired by his efforts were in the noble tradition of the beginnings of the collection.

In conjunction with the Harvard Tercentenary in 1936, a loan exhibition of art treasures from Japan, including pieces from the Imperial Palace, the Imperial Household Museum, and government institutions, was held at the Museum of Fine Arts. Then, as with the post-war exhibition of painting and sculpture sent to the United States by the Japanese government in 1953, the Korean exhibition of 1957, and the Chinese treasures from Taiwan that were circulating in 1961–62, visitors to the Museum of Fine Arts felt not so much a sense of novelty as the recognition of quality with which they were already long familiar from the museum's own permanent holdings.

In 1917 when Dr. Denman W. Ross gave the museum his large and varied collection of works of art, which included Indian bronzes, Jaina manuscripts, and Rajput and Maghal paintings, the first section dealing with the art of India in an American museum was created. Simultaneously, Dr. Ananda K. Coomaraswamy was brought to Boston as its keeper. This distinguished scholar, born in Ceylon and educated in England, who joined in his mind and inheritance the cultures of India and the West, remained at the Museum of Fine Arts until his death in 1947.

As early as 1872 the Museum of Fine Arts became con-cerned with Egypt when C. Granville Way gave a group of small objects and a number of mummies collected between 1824 and 1858 by the Englishman, Robert Hay. In 1875 the Way collection was joined by granite sculptures from the ruins of the great temple at Karnak acquired forty years earlier by John Lowell (1799–1836). This son of Francis Cabot Lowell, after the death of his wife and daughters from scarlet fever, had abandoned the textile business in 1831 and set out upon eastern travels from which he never returned. At Luxor in Upper Egypt he bought the Karnak sculptures; there also he fell ill and made a will establishing the Lowell Institute—of which more will be said later—which became effective when he died at Bombay.

As such gifts as these could not be counted upon for the building of a representative Egyptian collection, the museum turned to archaeology. From 1885 to 1905 it subscribed regu-larly to the excavations of the Egypt Exploration Fund (later known as the Egypt Exploration Society), a British research organization, in return for which support the museum re-ceived a substantial number of first-class objects. In 1905 the Harvard University—Museum of Fine Arts Egyptian Expe-dition was set up, with Dr. George A. Reisner as director, who for many years excavated in the region of the pyramids at Giza. Reisner, and his successors as curators of Egyptian Art at the museum, Dows Dunham and William Stevenson Smith, have over the past sixty years excavated not only at Giza, Gershesh, Amarna, Naga-ed-Dêr and other sites in Egypt, but at Kerma and the Cataract Forts, at Barkal, Kurri, Nuri, and the cemeteries of Meroë in the Sudan. Working under a concession from the Egyptian Government, the expedition was permitted to excavate and was obligated to publish scientific reports of the results in return for a share of the finds. In the earlier years when the finds were equally divided between the government and the excavators, the Museum of Fine Arts received remarkable additions to its Egyptian collections. But even in later years, when the development of nationalistic feeling reduced the number of objects permitted to leave the country, the Museum of Fine Arts continues to contribute to knowledge by the scholarly publications of its curators of Egyptian Art.

The Department of Classical Art derived its collections not from excavation but by purchase in the European market. For the decade following 1895, Edward Perry Warren (1860–1928), a Bostonian who, after Harvard and Oxford, had settled at Lewes in Sussex with the British-born John Marshall as secretary-companion, scoured the auction rooms and private collections of England and the Continent, seeking examples of classical art for the Museum of Fine Arts. Ninety-six pieces of sculpture were obtained in this period through Warren's and Marshall's activities, as well as coins, vases, and gems. This was pioneering work, for the Metropolitan Museum in New York did not enter the field seriously until ten or a dozen years later than Boston, while the other public collections are still younger.

As the museum in Copley Square was seen to be inadequate for collections growing at such a pace, the trustees in 1899 bought land in Huntington Avenue, on the edge of the Fenway. There in 1907–1909 the first section of a new building, designed by Guy Lowell, was constructed. In 1915 the

Robert Dawson Evans galleries for paintings, facing the Fenway and connected with the first building by a central wing, were completed. Thirteen years later a decorative arts wing was constructed to the eastward, thus achieving about three quarters of Guy Lowell's original plan. Paintings, prints, drawings, sculpture, furniture, decorative arts, textiles, books, and study materials of all kinds have increased at such pace that space is now very much at a premium. Since 1957 many of the painting and decorative arts galleries, as well as some of those devoted to the art of Egypt and India, have been handsomely renovated and re-installed. While that process continues, the time is approaching when the building must be extended to the limits of the land available.

The Museum of Fine Arts today offers something for every taste—ancient, medieval, or modern, Eastern or Western. By providing popular instruction through gallery talks, lectures, concerts, and television programs, it attracts three quarters of a million visitors each year, yet behind the scenes are curators whose scholarly production—especially in the Asiatic, Egyptian, and Classical departments—leave no doubt that this is also a learned institution, contributing to the advancement of knowledge. That collections of such magnitude and quality, supported by an endowment with a market value of over fifty million dollars, have been acquired in less than a century, entirely from private contributions, is in itself a reason for regarding Boston as a center of civilization.

Leaving the Museum of Fine Arts by the Fenway entrance, it is only three minutes' walk to the Isabella Stewart Gardner Museum, more briefly known as Fenway Court. This is the work of a single collector, maintained as she created it, and as such is as typical of the taste of the late nineteenth century as Sir John Soane's Museum in London is of its beginning.

Isabella Stewart (1840–1924), a New Yorker, married in 1860 the second John Lowell Gardner (1837–98), who had turned from his father's East India trade to western railroads and other business concerns in the United States. Soon after their marriage they settled in a brownstone Back Bay house at 152 Beacon Street, adding in 1880 the adjacent building at Number 150 to provide a music room. Their only child having died in infancy, Mrs. Gardner's very considerable energies were turned to travel, music, and enlivening what was often a rather unimaginative city. The Back Bay of the last quarter of the nineteenth century was handsome and comfortable, but always understated, sometimes stodgy, and rarely stylish. Mrs. Gardner had taste, style, imagination, and moved considerably faster than most of her contemporaries; hence a considerable mythology grew concerning her. She understood artists; Whistler, Sargent, and Zorn were her friends, as were numerous musicians.

Furnishing the new music room in the early eighties edged her into collecting, and on returning from Japan in 1884 by way of Europe, she became greatly absorbed in the glories of European painting. In Seville in 1888 she bought a Zurbarán Madonna, which whetted her taste for important pictures. In the nineties she seriously settled down to collecting works of art on a large scale. In this she was aided by Bernard Berenson (1865–1959), a brilliant Lithuanian Jew who had grown up in the slums of Boston, and whom she had helped to go to Italy after his graduation from Harvard College in 1887. Immersed in the study of Renaissance painting in Italy, Berenson often brought to Mrs. Gardner's attention paintings of major importance that could be bought—and were. Botticelli, Titian, Holbein, Tintoretto, and Rembrandt began to figure in her purchases; by 1896 it was apparent that the Beacon Street houses would not much longer accommodate the growing collection.

Mrs. Gardner's paintings were of all nationalities and ranged from Giotto to Matisse, but it is the Italian pictures that give the collection a unique character in the United States. Sir Philip Hendy, after cataloging the collection in the twenties observed: "The Uffizi Gallery at Florence, the Kaiser Friedrich Museum in Berlin, the National Gallery in London, and the Museum of the Louvre in Paris contain in an equally representative character incomparably greater wealth, but after these the collection at Fenway Court surpasses perhaps every wealthier museum in the extent of its representation of Italian painting."

In January, 1899, a few weeks after her husband's sudden death, Mrs. Gardner bought land in the Fenway for the construction of a future home for the collection. The house was built around a four-story glass-roofed courtyard in which were incorporated windows, balconies, columns, and other architectural elements from destroyed Venetian buildings. The first three stories were given over to great tall rooms of Italian proportions, suitable for the elegant display of the pictures; in her living quarters on the fourth floor, the familiar surroundings of her Beacon Street houses were closely reproduced. Although Fenway Court was, after Mrs. Gardner moved there in the winter of 1902–1903, often the scene of concerts and large parties that required the use of the lower floors, it had been planned for the future as a public institution. It was indeed "The Isabella Stewart Gardner Museum in the Fenway MDCCCC"—as a tablet (concealed by a marble slab until her death) over the main entrance read—rather than a grandiose private house.

The arrangement was dramatic and imaginative, rather than pedantically instructive. From every room one can look down into the courtyard filled with flowers from the greenhouses in Brookline. I saw the house only once in Mrs. Gardner's lifetime, when I was taken to a Christmas Eve midnight mass in the third floor chapel. The Gothic stained-glass window from St.-Denis that Henry Adams had procured for her was dark, but the adjacent Gothic Room, lit only by candles, with great logs blazing in the fireplace, was, like the view into the court, unforgettable. One felt that the house had grown over centuries rather than having been contrived, for things were where they looked well rather than where a conventional curator would put them.

After Mrs. Gardner's death on July 17, 1924, Fenway Court was opened, as her will directed, "as a Museum for the education and enjoyment of the public forever." The provision that forbade rearrangement, substitutions, additions, or changes in the collection seemed at the time unduly restrictive, but after forty years I am glad that she made it. Every other museum that I know has changed beyond recognition in these four decades, some of them for the worse. The finest pictures in Fenway Court would be worth seeing even if hung at eye level, flanked by aspidistras, on characterless walls lighted by fluorescent tubes screened by egg crates, with purple, green, and yellow chairs of eccentric shape for the convenience of visitors. But I like them better as they are, and because their arrangement remains unchanged, Fenway Court is not only a remarkable collection of pictures but an equally remarkable document in the history of taste at the turn of the nineteenth and twentieth centuries. And because Mrs. Gardner left ample endowment for its maintenance, there is an abundance of music and of flowers. Moreover, it is unique to have a museum that is not outgrowing its building and asking for contributions!

As with libraries, one cannot properly assess the resources of Boston without crossing the Charles River to observe the varied branches of Harvard University, which include museums of world renown in the fine arts, archaeology, ethnology, and natural history. The university's commitment to the fine arts began in 1874 when Charles Eliot Norton was appointed Lecturer on the History of the Fine Arts as Connected with Literature. This descriptive mouthful was altered the following year to Professor of the History of Art, a title that he bore actively until 1898 and as emeritus until his death ten years later. In 1894–95 the Fogg Art Museum was built within the college yard as a home for the department created by Norton.

On its completion, Francis Calley Gray's collection of prints was brought back from the Museum of Fine Arts; otherwise, it started nearly from scratch so far as original works of art were concerned. Within four years, however, Edward Waldo Forbes, Class of '95, a grandson of John Murray Forbes and Ralph Waldo Emerson, began to give and lend the museum important examples of Italian painting and classical sculpture. In 1909, Mr. Forbes started a forty-year term as director, during which he made the Fogg Art Museum what it is today. He was shortly joined by Paul J. Sachs, a distinguished collector of drawings, who had fallen so far under the spell of Charles Eliot Norton as an undergraduate that in 1915 he withdrew from the New York banking firm of Goldman, Sachs and Company to return to Cambridge; he settled in Norton's old house—Shady Hill—and gave the remainder of his active career to the Fogg Art Museum. This pair, very different in origins but very much alike in their passionate devotion to art collecting and to Harvard, themselves gave generously to the Fogg, both in objects and funds, and persuaded their numerous friends in New York and New England to follow their examples.

When I first knew the Fogg Museum as an undergraduate, it was so crowded that one literally put one's coat and hat on a case of Chinese porcelains and sat on a Romanesque capital for want of space elsewhere. In 1924, Bishop Lawrence and Professor Sachs—again a surprising but tremendously effective combination—went begging for ten million dollars on behalf of various branches of Harvard University. From this campaign came the present complex of the Graduate School of Business Administration, new chemistry laboratories, and a new and vastly larger Fogg Art Museum in Quincy Street, which was opened in 1927.

In the twenties Langdon Warner, Class of 1903, as Fellow of the Fogg Art Museum for Research in Asia, led expeditions to Western China, while Dr. Hetty Goldman excavated at Colophon in Asia Minor and Eutresis in Boeotia under the joint auspices of the Fogg and the American School of Classical Studies at Athens. Similarly, since 1958, Professor George

M. A. Hanfmann, curator of classical art, has been digging at Sardis under the joint aegis of the Fogg and Cornell University. Although important objects have come from these expeditions, the greater part of the museum's collections have been received by gifts and bequests of alumni and friends. The bequest of Grenville Lindall Winthrop, Class of '86, for example, included incredible riches in such varied fields as T'ang sculpture and French art of the eighteenth century.

The Fogg Art Museum today possesses original works of art—ancient, medieval, and modern, Eastern and Western—of high quality. Their variety is best seen in the occasional picture books illustrating acquisitions, recently inaugurated by the present director, Professor John Coolidge. Although the collections are an aid to university teaching rather than an end in themselves, they are freely open at all times to visitors from outside the university. Even with the infinitely greater collections of the Museum of Fine Arts just across the river, there are objects in almost any field that justify a visit to the Fogg.

Also under Professor Coolidge's direction, although housed in an attractive building of its own at the corner of Kirkland Street and Divinity Avenue, is the Busch-Reisinger Museum of Germanic Culture. Springing from the gift by Kaiser Wilhelm II in 1900 of plaster casts of German sculpture, the museum has, under the curatorship of Professor Charles L. Kuhn, acquired various original works of modern German art. German music of the baroque period has gained increased popularity through the use by E. Power Biggs and other musicians of the organ installed in 1958 in the Romanesque Hall of the Busch-Reisinger Museum. This instrument, constructed by D. A. Flentrop of Zaandam in Holland, has been described as the first "true-classic" organ in the United States in that it continues and develops the art of organ building as practiced by Arp Schnitger and others in the seventeenth century.

A few steps up Divinity Avenue brings one to the Peabody Museum of Archaeology and Ethnology, founded in 1866 through a gift of George Peabody of London. Although this institution, which was the first definitely anthropological museum in the United States, is as intertwined with the department of anthropology as the Fogg Art Museum is with the teaching of the fine arts, there is an important difference, pointed out by the late Professor Roland B. Dixon: "In most branches of learning that are pursued in Harvard University, laboratories, museums, and libraries are the outgrowth of teaching and research. In anthropology, the order is reversed; and for the obvious reason that anthropology is so young a science that the overwhelming need was to discover and classify data, rather than to present conclusions which were purely tentative. Most of the significant history of anthropology has occurred since the Peabody Museum was founded in 1866."

And for much of it the Peabody Museum has helped to provide data and evidence. Although a professorship in American Archaeology and Ethnology—now held by John Otis Brew, the present director of the museum—was endowed by George Peabody, the institution has never limited itself geographically. It has excavated in Ohio, the Mississippi Valley, the Southwest, Mexico, Guatemala, and Peru. Members of its staff make themselves quite at home among the pygmies of the Kalahari Desert of southwest Africa and in the jungles of New Guinea and the Solomon Islands. They dig at Les Eyzies in the Dordogne, measure skulls in the Caucasus, and collect masks in Liberia. All of this activity throughout the world swells the exhibition cases and storerooms, and eventually the publications, of the Peabody Museum.

While some collections of the Peabody Museum would be intelligible only to the scholar, others—especially examples of Maya sculpture and pre-Colombian gold—are of extraordinary beauty. A layman could, for example, also learn more about European pre-history than would be possible from books by examining the objects and reading the labels in certain galleries. Moreover, the museum's Film Study Center, of which Robert G. Gardner is director, produces from miles of documentary footage of the lives of present-day survivals of stone age culture—as in New Guinea and the Kalahari Desert—films of extraordinary beauty and general interest. By one of the typical quirks of Boston, Mr. Gardner's laboratories, containing such a record of primitive man, are, for greater convenience, housed in the cement fortress known as the Visual Arts Center (adjoining the Fogg) that is the only example of Le Corbusier's architecture in the United States.

The Peabody Museum occupies one wing of a great factory-like open quadrangle extending from Divinity Avenue to Oxford Street that is in large part devoted to the Museum of Comparative Zoology. This is the offspring of the Swiss scientist, Louis Agassiz (1807–73), who, coming to Harvard in 1847, created a great scientific institution out of nothing during the fifties and sixties. With an evangelical fervor for the biological sciences quite as great as his intellectual attainments in them, Agassiz collected specimens and begged money for the establishment of a museum of natural history. His opportunity came in 1858 when the university placed at his disposal fifty thousand dollars bequeathed by Francis Calley Gray in addition to his collection of prints. The funds were accompanied by a condition that the building be called the Museum of Comparative Zoology. By this accident, what is in fact a greater general museum of natural history became saddled with a cumbersome name that neither suggests its origin nor its activities.

The building was begun in 1859, but completed later in the century through the generosity of the founder's son, Alexander Agassiz (1835–1910), who, in addition to a distinguished career as a zoologist, oceanographer, and as director of the museum, also achieved a fortune through his management of the Calumet copper mines in northern Michigan. Thomas Barbour, who became director in 1927, recalled how Alexander Agassiz went so regularly from the museum to the Calumet and Hecla Mining Company office in Ashburton Place in Boston, "driving in and out in a brougham with a very good-looking pair of horses," that you could set your clock by the arrival and departure of his carriage. Alexander Agassiz's brother-in-law, Theodore Lyman (1833–97), whose example led to the tradition that one should work for the Museum of Comparative Zoology without stipend if one could possibly afford to do so, contributed both to the solvency and learning of the institution. As treasurer he did much to put its affairs on a sound basis; as a volunteer scientist he became the world authority on the taxonomy of the group of the brittle stars, or Ophiuroidea.

The Agassizs, father and son, had no patience with the

eighteenth-century notion of a "cabinet of natural and artificial curiosities." In their museum every room, every case, every specimen should be there for a definite reason in order to play its role, however small, in the universal drama of natural history. As collecting, research, publication, and teaching were inextricably interwoven in the plan, the exhibits, however extensive, were only part of the museum. The stimulating atmosphere of the institution has, over the years, induced many New Englanders to follow Theodore Lyman's example in giving their services as curators, thus converting a personal interest into a highly professional contribution to learning. By such means the research activities of the Museum of Comparative Zoology have long been strengthened and accelerated.

As with an iceberg, whose visible masses give no clue to what may be lurking under water, research museums have far more below the surface than meets the eye. While the Harvard scientific museums cannot, and should not, give lavish space to window-dressing techniques of exhibition, their public galleries have long afforded instruction to any visitor with a desire to learn. Harvard's botanical resources, in two very different forms, have long inspired popular enthusiasm and admiration. The "glass flowers" in the Botanical Museum, blown in the last century by Leopold and Rudolph Blaschka, father and son, at Meissen in Germany, were designed to provide a synoptic collection of realistic representations of plant-life in tolerably permanent form. They have also been objects of wonder and curiosity to hundreds of thousands of visitors over seventy years. Some of these sight-seers, of course, would have been equally entranced by a two-headed calf. The hundreds of thousands who have visited the Arnold Arboretum in Jamaica Plain have, on the contrary, been drawn rather by a love of beauty, for this area, which is largely due to the imagination and energy of Professor Charles Sprague Sargent (1841–1927), offers an unrivaled sequence of flowering trees and shrubs, planted on a charmingly diversified terrain.

This institution, created in 1872 through a bequest of the New Bedford merchant James Arnold, and established on land in West Roxbury left the University by Benjamin Bussey, was designed to contain all the trees, shrubs, and herbaceous plants, indigenous or exotic, that could be raised there in the open air. In the eighties, when Frederick Law Olmsted was designing the Boston park system, the land was conveyed to the city of Boston for inclusion in Olmsted's plan. It was then leased back to the University for a thousand years at an annual rent of one dollar, with an agreement by which the city provided roadways, policing, and water in return for the Arnold Arboretum being open for public inspection as a limited area of the park system. The trees and hardy shrubs, which are arranged by families and genera in as essentially natural a sequence as the varied terrain permits, represent whatever natives of the cool temperate parts of North America, Europe, and Asia will survive in the region of Boston.

From the beginning Professor Sargent constantly attempted to enlarge the horticultural horizons of the United States by extensive collecting abroad; by 1922 the Arnold Arboretum had 1,286 kinds of woody plants, brought for the first time into cultivation. In 1892, Sargent visited Japan and established exchange relations with botanists there. Ernest H. Wilson of the Arboretum staff explored many parts of the world, discovering and obtaining, especially in western China, seeds or living specimens of many species and varieties never before cultivated, many of which were wholly new to science. When Wilson's discoveries domesticated themselves happily in the Arboretum and proved suitable for decorative planting, Professor Sargent would make stock available to nurserymen for propagation and sale. Many of the handsomest flowering trees, shrubs, and plants that now adorn American gardens and parks are Chinese immigrants, naturalized through the energies and imagination of Wilson and Sargent. The Arnold Arboretum is a delight to those who visit it; it has also brought beauty to hundreds of thousands of gardens whose owners may never have realized how this institution has enlarged the horizons of horticulture.

Just as the Massachusetts Historical Society was founded in 1791, long before colleges had concerned themselves formally with American history, so the Boston Society of Natural History, organized in 1830, was the first institution in New England in its field. As one of its original members observed: "There was not a college in New England, excepting Yale, where philosophical geology of the modern school was taught. There was not a work extant by a New England author which presumed to group the geological structure of any portion of our territory of greater extent than a county. There was not in existence a bare catalogue, to say nothing of a general history, of the animals of Massachusetts, of any class. There was not within our borders a single museum of Natural History founded according to the requirements and based upon the system of modern science, nor a single journal advocating exclusively its interests."

In its early decades the museum and publications of the Boston Society of Natural History pioneered, but, as the Museum of Comparative Zoology developed, they gradually came to duplicate, in less extensive form, what was available four miles away. With increasing ease in moving back and forth across the Charles River, this came to make less and less sense, particularly as many of the more distinguished officers and curators of the society were also members of the Harvard family. The society's museum, built in the eighteen sixties in the new Back Bay, had, by the early twentieth century, degenerated into chaos. Dr. Thomas Barbour recalled it as "apparently a studied effort to demonstrate what a museum should not be," observing that: "The exhibits were so dingy, so overcrowded, and, I may add, so revolting, that it was widely rumored that recalcitrant children of the families living in the Back Bay were dragged in and walked through the Natural History Rooms to strike terror to their hearts as a bitter and long-to-be-remembered punishment."

General housecleaning, begun in the nineteen twenties, resulted in the eventual transformation of the society into the sponsors of an entirely popular Museum of Science, housed since 1951 in a new building overlooking the Charles River Basin in an area called—to me, at least, rather horridly—Science Park. With this metamorphosis, the learned activities and research collections of the organization went into abeyance. Under the direction of the mountaineer Bradford Washburn, the Museum of Science has become an effective instrument for popular indoctrination in industrial as well as natural history, handsomely housed, complete with planetarium. It emphasizes school visits and lecture-demonstration programs, courses for children, young people, and adults. Designed solely for children are the separate, privately-maintained Children's Museum in Jamaica Plain and the Children's Art Centre on Rutland Street in the South End.

Since 1881 the Bostonian Society has occupied the city-owned Old State House at the intersection of Washington and State streets. In its earlier years it published sixteen volumes of studies in local history in addition to an annual volume of *Proceedings*; of late its chief function has been that of maintaining a museum of Boston history in quarters that are much too small. At present it is in a state of deliberately suspended animation, for it is anticipated that the National Park Service will in the near future undertake the restoration and operation of the Old State House. When this occurs, the Bostonian Society will seek larger quarters elsewhere—hopefully in the present City Hall, which will in a few years become vacant—and attempt to create there a Boston equivalent of the Musée Carnavalet or the London Museum.

The Institute of Contemporary Art, the Guild of Boston Artists, and the galleries of art dealers offer a considerable variety of changing picture exhibitions in the length of Newbury Street, as does the Print Department of the Boston Public Library, around the corner in Copley Square.

Half an hour away in Salem is another Peabody Museum which specializes in maritime history, ethnology, and the natural history of Essex County. By carrying on the collections of the Salem East India Marine Society, founded in 1799, it counts as the oldest museum in continuous operation in the United States. It also inherited from that source a contemporary record of the great period of New England seafaring, memorabilia of the China trade, and ethnological objects from Pacific islands, collected so early that they represent Polynesian culture in its uncontaminated state. Through Edward S. Morse's long directorship, and the generosity of Dr. Charles G. Weld and other Japanese-minded Bostonians, the Peabody Museum of Salem built up a unique collection of Japanese ethnology that supplements the paintings and sculpture in the Museum of Fine Arts and affords a picture of the pre-European life of Japan, unrivaled there or elsewhere. In Salem, too, is the Essex Institute, the most remarkable county historical society in the United States in the richness of its manuscripts and its century-long record of continuous scholarly publication, which maintains a museum and a group of historic houses.

Organizations concerned with some aspect of history or historic preservation in Boston are almost as numerous as dining clubs, but as most of them are administered by men having close ties with one or more of the older learned societies, their fields of activity follow an orderly and non-competitive pattern.

The Society for the Preservation of New England Antiquities, founded in 1910 by William Sumner Appleton, has from private funds acquired and maintained some fifty properties in various parts of New England. Its headquarters are in the Bulfinch house at 141 Cambridge Street that is the sole survival of the great houses of the late eighteenth and early nineteenth century that once clustered about Bowdoin Square in the West End. In addition to the work of the S.P.N.E.A., numerous independent charitable corporations, organized for the purpose, preserve Boston monuments like the Old South Meeting House, the Old Corner Book Store, the Paul Revere and Hichborn houses in the North End. But for every building of historical or architectural interest in Boston that is preserved for exhibition, there are many more that survive through some adaptive use, whether private or institutional. In this phase of historic preservation, even learned societies of purely scientific purposes have a hand, for the American Meteorological Association maintains its national headquarters at 45 Beacon Street in the last of the three great houses that Charles Bulfinch designed for Harrison Gray Otis.

Within the orbit of Boston are innumerable other historic houses owned by the Society for the Preservation of New England Antiquities, the Trustees of Reservations, local historical societies, or non-profit corporations organized for the preservation of such buildings as Craigie House in Cambridge, Gore Place in Waltham, or John Greenleaf Whittier's birthplace in Haverhill. Collectively these constitute an extraordinary representation of the architecture and decorative arts of the region.

Within easy reach, too, are the Addison Gallery of American Art at Phillips Academy in Andover, and the Fruitlands Museum, on a dramatic hillside in the town of Harvard, which deals with Transcendentalists, Shakers, local Indians, and portraits by itinerant painters. Altogether, the museums of Boston provide nourishment that is quite as catholic as that afforded by the libraries.

VIII

Learning

HARVARD COLLEGE, as every literate person knows, was founded not in Boston but in Cambridge, yet several of its graduate schools are settled on the Boston side of the Charles River, and Boston men have long played major roles in the policies of the entire university. Although the Harvard Medical School began in Cambridge in 1782, since all its early professors, save Benjamin Waterhouse, lived and practiced medicine in Boston, the school moved there in 1810. With the establishment of the Massachusetts General Hospital, it became anchored there for good. Thus the medical faculty has long been physically separated from the rest of the university. Although the Graduate School of Business Administration and the college's playing fields are within the Boston city limits, they are set off from most of Harvard only by an adequately bridged river. Nevertheless, Boston long had a hand in the affairs of Harvard that was far more decisive than the proportion of university activities located within its limits might suggest.

On October 28, 1636, the General Court of the Massachusetts Bay Colony passed a vote agreeing to give four hundred pounds towards a college, "and the next Court to appoint wheare and what building." We have already seen how this—the first collegiate establishment in British North America—

soon came to be named in honor of its earliest benefactor, the Reverend John Harvard. In 1650, for the better government of the young institution, the General Court issued a charter creating the President, five Fellows, and the Treasurer a corporation to be called the President and Fellows of Harvard College, with "perpetual succession." This seven-man corporation, after more than three centuries, is still the senior governing body. The President and Fellows of Harvard College are the oldest corporation in North America operating under their original charter, and in local parlance are simply referred to as "the Corporation."

The five Fellows were originally conceived of as resident teachers, like those in any English collegiate establishment. So was the President until the election in 1685 of the Reverend Increase Mather, minister of the Second Church in Boston, who assumed the post without giving up his Boston pulpit or residence. This cross-river commuting left so much to be desired that, after fifteen years, the General Court required Mather to be one thing or the other. After he had tried living six months in Cambridge, he resigned the presidency in 1701 and went back to his church. By a neat bit of political double-thinking, the Reverend Samuel Willard, minister of the Old South Church in Boston, took over the administration of the college, with the title of Vice-president, while retaining his Boston church and home. In the summer of 1707, Vice-president Willard, having been taken ill, resigned his duties at the college. The following autumn, with the election of John Leverett, Harvard College secured not only its first resident president in twenty-two years, but the first layman to hold the office.

Under the charter of 1650, for the first century and a quarter, the five Fellows of Harvard College had always been resident tutors, save during a part of President Leverett's administration when neighboring clergymen had been elected. This tradition was radically broken with the election in 1779 of the Boston merchant and Revolutionary statesman, James Bowdoin (1726–90), who was later to become the second governor of Massachusetts under the Constitution. The precedent set by Bowdoin's election was strengthened in 1784 by the choice of a second "solid citizen" of Boston, neither pedagogical nor clerical, Judge John Lowell (1743–1802), who served for eighteen years until his death. Thus the administration began to pass from Cambridge to Boston as the Corporation was transformed from a resident group of teachers to an external board of trustees. The process was complete by the second decade of the nineteenth century, for the death in 1806 of Eliphalet Pearson, Hancock Professor of Hebrew from 1786 and a Fellow from 1800, removed the last teacher regularly elected to the Corporation.

Because in this self-perpetuating body of seven the Fellows elected their successors, as well as the president, once a pattern was set it did not easily change. For the past century and a half, with but a few very recent exceptions, the Fellows of Harvard College have been Bostonians—normally merchants, lawyers, or bankers, with an occasional clergyman, public figure, or man of letters. In the early nineteenth century they were generally Unitarians and Federalists, that is, liberal in religion and conservative in politics. But as they cared little for sectarianism or political expediency and chiefly sought excellence wherever they could find it, the combination proved to be a good one.

For ninety-four of the hundred and forty-nine years following the election of Judge John Lowell as a Fellow of Harvard College, he or one of his direct descendants was a member of the Corporation. His son John Lowell (1769–1840), also a lawyer, was a Fellow from 1810 to 1822; his grandson John Amory Lowell (1798–1881), a textile manufacturer, was a Fellow from 1837 to 1877, while his great-great-grandson, Abbott Lawrence Lowell (1856–1943), was president from 1909 to 1933. The "Old Judge's" son, the Reverend Charles Lowell (1782–1861) was a Fellow in 1818, while a great-great-grandson, Judge Francis Cabot Lowell (1856–1911) served in the same capacity from 1895 until his death. John Amory Lowell's term of forty years was the longest of any Fellow in the nineteenth or twentieth centuries; it was only exceeded by that of the Reverend Henry Flynt who was a resident tutor from 1699 to 1754 and Fellow for the first sixty years of the eighteenth century! While Lowells have turned up with the greatest frequency, other families have been represented on the Corporation over long periods of time. The father of Charles William Eliot, president from 1869 to 1909, Samuel Atkins Eliot (1798–1862), had been treasurer from 1842 to 1853. Similarly, Charles Francis Adams, treasurer from 1898 to 1929, was the son of John Quincy Adams, Fellow from 1877 to 1894.

Twice in the nineteenth century, members of the Corporation were appointed professors while retaining their fellowships. Joseph Story, Fellow from 1825 to 1845, was Dane Professor of Law from 1829 to 1845, while James Walker, Fellow from 1834 to 1853, was also a professor from 1838 to 1853 and president from 1853 to 1860. Only once, however, was a resident teacher elected to the Corporation. For some reason not apparent at this distance, Ephraim W. Gurney, Professor of History, was, two years before his death in 1886, also made a Fellow of Harvard College. The historian Francis Parkman, whose only teaching had been in a professorship of horticulture (1871–72)—to which he had been led by an enthusiasm for rose-growing—was on the Corporation from 1875 to 1888. The scientist Alexander Agassiz, a Fellow in 1878–84 and 1886–90, and Bishop Lawrence, who was elected in 1913 and resigned in 1931, were as astute financiers as their colleagues who were completely rooted in State Street.

Next to John Amory Lowell's forty years, the longest terms of service have been those of Dr. Henry Pickering Walcott (1890–1927) and of the lawyer Thomas Nelson Perkins, who was a Fellow for thirty of the years between 1905 and his death in 1937. In the mid-twenties Nelson Perkins took a couple of years off for government service in connection with the Dawes Plan and the Reparations Commission.

The Fellows of Harvard College have two distinctive traits: a capacity for hard work and a fondness for anonymity. They meet fortnightly to consider not only financial matters but all teaching appointments involving permanent tenure. While they know a great deal about the various faculties, the faculty members sometimes hardly know who the Fellows are, for their only public ceremonial appearance is to flank the President on the Commencement platform, where there are enough top hats and morning coats—sometimes rented—on other people to give them protective coloration. I have introduced a Fellow and a professor—both friends of mine and members of the same club— who did not know each other by sight. They got on well, and I had the impression that each felt better about the world for discovering the intellectual quality and pleasant manners of the other.

Most important of all, the Corporation, in picking presidents, seems to have a deal of inspiration in choosing the right type of man for the era, both of Harvard and of the country. In 1869 and 1933 they chose chemists; in 1909 a Lowell lawyer who taught government; in 1953 an Iowa-born classicist. The qualities of Presidents Eliot, Lowell, Conant, and Pusey were suited to their times. No one of them would necessarily have done so well in the time of any other. And at least in the two elections within my memory, the Corporation has picked unexpected dark horses with good wind and legs. Nobody would have predicted James B. Conant or Nathan M. Pusey as obvious candidates in 1933 and 1953. In making such choices, and in steering an inspired course between the Scylla of the left and Charybdis of the right, lie two of the singular merits of the Harvard Corporation as reconstituted in the early nineteenth century. A third, and highly useful virtue, is the knowledge of what to do with money.

In this latter respect the Boston trustee is singularly at home. When Edward William Hooper (1839–1901), the father of Mrs. Henry Adams, retired in 1898 after twenty-two years as treasurer of Harvard College, President Eliot paid this tribute to his stewardship: "It appears ... that the number of funds and balances in the Treasurer's books increased during the twenty-two years by 243 per cent; that the amounts of these funds and balances increased 325 per cent; that the gain on property bought by Mr. Hooper, partly sold but chiefly held, was a million dollars; that the surplus of the estimated cash value of the general investments over their book value increased between 1876 and 1898 from 5 per cent to 16 per cent; and that the estimated increase, excluding gifts, in the value of the property now belonging to the general investments, was a million and a quarter dollars. The President and Fellows declared, and put on record, their opinion that the University rests under lasting obligations to Mr. Hooper for greatly increasing its property in spite of adverse conditions and troublous times, and for inspiring throughout the community a well-grounded confidence in its financial management—an opinion in which all the alumni and friends of the University heartily unite."

Friends of the University have had good cause for equal confidence in the management of Mr. Hooper's successors, Charles Francis Adams, Henry Lee Shattuck, William H. Claflin, Paul Codman Cabot, and the present incumbent, George F. Bennett. They have done so well that Mr. Cabot, in a 1963 article entitled "Chasing the Budget, My Twelve Years as Treasurer," undertook to explain that Harvard is not really as rich as it seems to the uninformed. He began: "It is with considerable reluctance that I am persuaded to write about Harvard's money. This reluctance stems from a concern that what I propose to say might be misinterpreted. I know that some people have either entirely refrained from giving to Harvard, or minimized their gift because of their belief that 'Harvard is the richest university in the country.' As far as I know, this is true. Harvard is the richest, at least in terms

148

of the market value of its endowment funds, but there are other valid and true facts bearing on this subject which must be considered and which I propose to set forth. In brief:

"—If our endowment funds had not increased very materially over the years, the custodianship and management of the funds entrusted to us would not merit the confidence of donors. Without good and careful management we would not get, nor deserve to get, those gifts which have made our operations possible.

"—Although both principal and income of our endowment funds have grown materially, they do not pay for as large a per cent of our expenses as they did in the past.

"—Our needs have grown enormously, and perhaps can best be expressed by what we do *not* have and cannot now afford, but need and want badly."

On the first point, a table demonstrated how Harvard's investments grew from $10,468,000 in 1901 to $73,786,000 in 1932; from $203,881,000 in 1948 to $709,415,000 in 1962. By the time of Mr. Cabot's retirement in 1965, they had passed the one billion mark. Since 1932 the amount of common stocks has very greatly increased, while investment real estate has practically disappeared. On the second point, Mr. Cabot warned that, although investment income availed of during the period from 1948 to 1962 rose from $6,600,000 to $19,900,000, in 1948 it met 25 per cent of the university's total expenses, whereas in 1962 it met only 21.7 per cent.

"This is merely [he writes] another way of saying that although endowment income increased 201 per cent, expenses during this period increased even faster—230 per cent."

The latter increase meant in 1962 a budget of $88,500,000 a

year rather than the $26,600,000 that prevailed when Mr. Cabot took office in 1948. During the academic year 1963-64, although expenses mounted to $110,000,000, total income rose 11.7 per cent to $115,000,000. Despite the handsome increase in dollars, the income received from returns on endowment amounted to only 20.4 per cent of the year's budget.

One realizes that the vastly increased budget goes to the best possible uses when one notes that during President Pusey's first decade in office the teaching and research staff in the Faculty of Arts and Sciences grew from 971 to 1,438, while the enrolment of degree candidates only increased from 7,020 to 8,375. To have 40 per cent more professors available in this one faculty augments and diversifies the intellectual fare, while the rise in scholarship and loan funds throughout the university of $2,760,000 (excluding government money) in 1953-54 to $7,654,000 in 1962-63 makes learning more readily available. The ten-year total spent for scholarships and loans amounts to $56,395,200, of which $49,761,200 was from Harvard funds, privately given, and only $6,634,000 from government sources.

Until after World War I, the Harvard Corporation consisted exclusively of resident Bostonians. In the past forty years a few New Yorkers have slipped in, and one Baltimorean. This local quality is due not so much to a Bostonian self-sufficiency as to the frequency of meetings and the detail of work to be accomplished. The college seeks its students nationally; sons of alumni, particularly Bostonians, are no longer necessarily welcome if they appear on registration day. Only if they possess qualities that will stand up to national competition do they have a chance of admission. But the Corporation necessarily still hails from the eastern seaboard.

At Commencement, 1965, the senior and junior Fellows, Charles A. Coolidge and Francis H. Burr, were partners in the Boston law firm of Ropes and Gray, where Nelson Perkins practiced. The others were R. Keith Kane, a New York lawyer, and William L. Marbury, a Baltimorean of the same profession, and Thomas S. Lamont, vice-chairman of the board of directors of the Morgan Guaranty Trust Company. The treasurer was pure Boston, in name as well as experience. Forty-one years ago Paul Cabot became treasurer of the State Street Investment Corporation and thirty-one years ago its president; since 1958 he has been chairman of its board of directors.

In reference to his activities as treasurer of Harvard College, he wrote: "One of our fiscal safeguards is the State Street Research and Management Company, which has for many years supplied investment advice and management to the State Street Investment Corporation. When I was elected Treasurer of Harvard, it was at first suggested that I resign my position as partner in this company. This I refused to do for many reasons, but largely because I felt that giving up the aid of the research organization that I had helped create would be like asking a carpenter to come to work without his tools. Harvard thereupon agreed to retain (for a nominal figure) the services of the State Street Research and Management Company, and the arrangement continues."

On July 1, 1965, Messrs. Coolidge and Cabot retired. A. L. Nickerson became the junior Fellow, while Mr. Cabot was succeeded by George F. Bennett, president of the State Street Investment Corporation since 1958. Mr. Nickerson's appointment reduces the lawyers in the group from four to three, for since his graduation in 1933 he has been continuously with the Socony Mobil Oil Company. Joining that firm as a service station attendant, he rose to be its president, and since 1951 chairman of its board. Financially speaking, Messrs. Cabot and Bennett are cut off the same piece of goods. The new treasurer, however, represents a theological innovation, for he is a Deacon of the South Shore Baptist Church. He is, I believe, the first Baptist member of the Harvard Corporation since President Henry Dunster was turned out of office in 1654 for his adoption of the tenents of that sect. Of his "apostasy," Samuel Eliot Morison has written: "The news that President Dunster had become an 'amtipaedobaptist' created much the same sensation in New England as would be aroused in the country today if President Conant should announce his adherence to communism. Baptists were regarded by other Christians at that time much as are the communists of our day by adherents of the capitalist order. They were disturbers of the peace and enemies of our institutions."

Tempers have cooled in regard to religious belief since the seventeenth century. Baptists, like Quakers, are no longer regarded as "disturbers of the peace"; that they are no longer "enemies of our institutions" is indicated by the confidence placed in one of them 311 years after President Dunster was sacked.

The quality of mind that members of the Harvard Corporation bring to their exacting but essentially anonymous tasks may best be seen in an essay that Charles A. Coolidge wrote shortly before his retirement after thirty years' service on that board. After pointing out that the governing boards do at most 10 per cent of the job of governing Harvard, he offered a few rules of conduct which he summarized "by a big 'don't'—*don't meddle*."

"Don't try to impose your pet theory of education [he continues.] Resist harking back to your own college days and urging changes in the curriculum which you now think, through the rosy glasses of nostalgia, would have made you into an avid scholar. Because son Johnny has done well at an ultramodern school, don't advocate the abolition of all exams. Because at your latest Class reunion you heard a snappy lecture on a subject of current interest, don't urge that the classics be dropped.

"In short, you must realize that you are not an expert in education. Accompanying this realization should be an appreciation of what a difficult and delicate matter it is to make wise decisions in higher education. I remember as a boy being enthralled by tales of Indians who could follow a trail by a crumpled leaf or a bent twig. They had developed a sixth sense. In my opinion, a sixth sense is needed today to keep on the trail through the forest of higher education. It is needed to spot and analyze the problems, and to decide them in a way that will lead to progress. And I am sure that a sixth sense in this field requires an academic background. No layman, however competent, can hope to acquire the essential delicacy of perception and nice sense of values.

"As I see it, the job of a lay member of a governing board such as the Corporation boils down to this. Do your best to see that the organization is good, that it is well manned, and that it runs smoothly—but don't try to run it. Make your decisions on evidence furnished you by experts, and not on your own imperfect knowledge of academic matters. If you do that, I think you will be of real help to the President, and that in my view is what you are there for."

If there is a better rule of conduct for a trustee of any learned institution, I have yet to find it. Mr. Coolidge's remarks could well be pondered and adopted far outside Boston.

The Boston that has produced such a line of trustees and treasurers has not confined itself to balance sheets on the Harvard scene; it has contributed its share of teachers and scholars as well as administrators. As we have earlier seen, Charles William Eliot, springing from a line of Boston merchants, preferred teaching mathematics and chemistry to managing textile mills. As President of Harvard from 1869 to 1909, he not only transformed a New England college into a great university, in the German style, but he exercised a unique influence on education in the United States. His successor, Abbott Lawrence Lowell, the grandson of the textile men Abbott Lawrence and John Amory Lowell, practiced law in Boston for seventeen years before turning to the teaching of government at Harvard. To Eliot's German university, he introduced many of the collegiate virtues of the older English universities, focusing the social and intellectual life of undergraduates in seven residential houses, patterned on English colleges.

Elizabeth Cabot Cary Agassiz (1822–1907), granddaughter of the China trade merchant Thomas Handasyd Perkins, and wife of the scientist Louis Agassiz, began in 1879 the "Society for the Collegiate Instruction of Women" that ultimately became Radcliffe College, of which she was the first president. "Anchored against the whole teaching force of Harvard," Radcliffe in fact, although not always in theory, has made Harvard co-educational. Mrs. Agassiz's creation offers unique advantages, for no independent women's college, however distinguished, can ever rival the resources of the Harvard faculty, libraries, and museums, that are available to Radcliffe students.

In the Harvard Corporation several generations of Boston families have demonstrated similar administrative and financial talents. In the faculty, Boston fathers and sons sometimes achieve scholarly distinction in quite different fields. For example, a physicist, the second Theodore Lyman (1874–1954), son of the zoologist, was long director of the Jefferson Physical Laboratory and discovered the "Lyman Series" of lines in the ultraviolet spectrum of atomic hydrogen, which paved the way for Niels Bohr's development in 1913 of the quantum theory of atomic structure. Elliot Forbes, today Fanny Peabody Mason Professor of Music and director of the Harvard Glee Club, is a son of Edward Waldo Forbes, long director of the Fogg Art Museum. The architectural historian John Coolidge, who succeeded Mr. Forbes at the Fogg, is a son of Julian Lowell Coolidge (1873–1954), professor of mathematics, and the first Master of Lowell House (1930–40). That first Master's older brother, the historian Archibald Cary Coolidge, set the Harvard library on the path to greatness. Julian Coolidge's successor at Lowell House, the historian Elliott Perkins, master from 1940 to 1963, is a son of the lawyer Thomas Nelson Perkins, who was a member of the Corporation for thirty years. A grandson and namesake of the chemist-president, Charles William Eliot, is today professor of city and regional planning.

Close ties with Boston do not necessarily limit the range of interest of some members of the Harvard faculty. The first recipient of the history prize of the Balzan Foundation—comparable in distinction to a Nobel Prize in the sciences—was Samuel Eliot Morison, who still lives in the Boston house at 44 Brimmer Street that was his birthplace in 1887. Having begun his career as the historian of Federalist Boston, maritime Massachusetts, and Harvard College, Mr. Morison became the sea-going biographer of Christopher Columbus and the historian of United States naval operations in World War II, retiring with the rank of rear admiral. Nor are such ties between Boston and the Harvard faculty exclusively of earlier generations, for McGeorge Bundy—even though a Yale graduate—a great-nephew of President A. Lawrence Lowell, became Dean of the Faculty of Arts and Sciences in 1953 at the age of thirty-four, resigning in 1961 to become President Kennedy's special assistant for national security.

Harvard College was first designated a university in 1780 when John Adams drafted the constitution of Massachusetts. In the course of the next year it became one in fact as well as name by the creation of the Harvard Medical School. The Law School was established in 1817, the Divinity School two years later, thus providing, in addition to traditional instruction in the liberal arts, separate faculties for training in the recognized professions. But the Industrial Revolution soon created the need for the new profession of engineering. When the Lawrence Scientific School was created in 1847, Abbott Lawrence, the benefactor for whom it was named, and other Boston merchants and manfacturers like him, thought they were to see a technical school for the professional training of engineers who would be useful to the expanding industry of New England.

The arrival that very year of Louis Agassiz, who swept all before him, frustrated their hopes. Agassiz's appointment as professor of zoology and geology diverted all Harvard's scientific efforts from applied to pure fields; thus the Lawrence Scientific School became a place for individual study and research in zoology and geology rather than a nursery for budding engineers. Instruction in the applied sciences was eventually to come, not from Harvard but from an independent organization, the Massachusetts Institute of Technology, that grew up in the new Back Bay and was, for its first half century, entirely based in Boston.

The Swiss Louis Agassiz only married a Bostonian, Elizabeth Cabot Cary—his second wife—three years after he became a Harvard professor. By contrast, a Boston girl had a good deal to do with the presence in Boston of William Barton Rogers, the Virginia-born founder of the Massachusetts Institute of Technology. A geologist who was a professor at the University of Virginia, Rogers came to New England in the summer of 1845 to visit the White Mountains. Incidentally he met Emma, the daughter of the Boston banker-historian James Savage, whom he married four years later and took back to Charlottesville. In 1853, Rogers resigned his professorship at the University of Virginia and brought his wife back to Boston, settling in with the Savages in Temple Place, across the street, incidentally, from Mrs. Agassiz's parents, the Carys.

Rogers was one of four brothers, all remarkable for their scientific achievement. Another of them, Henry Darwin Rogers, who became Regius Professor of Natural History and Geology at Glasgow in 1855, had in 1846 drawn up a plan for a polytechnic school to be attached to the Lowell Institute in Boston: "A school of practical science completely organized should, I conceive, embrace full courses of instruction in all the principles of physical truth having direct relation to the art of constructing machinery, the application of motive power, manufactures, mechanical and chemical, the art of engraving with electrotype and photography, mineral exploration and mining, chemical analysis, engineering, locomotion, and agriculture." After setting forth specific examples in various fields, the report concluded: "A polytechnic school, therefore, duly organized, has in view an object of the utmost practical value, and one in which such a community as that of Boston could not fail of being realized in the amplest degree."

Although not accepted by John Amory Lowell, the sole trustee of his cousin John's benefaction, Henry Rogers's plan proved to be the blueprint for his brother's creation. From the time of his move to Boston, William Barton Rogers was constantly working towards the establishment of such a school. The first significant step was the passage of an "Act to Incorporate the Massachusetts Institute of Technology," which was approved by Governor John A. Andrew on April 10, 1861. Thus a great scientific institution, created by a Virginian, was incorporated by the Massachusetts legislature just two days before Fort Sumter was fired upon.

Because of the war, fund raising and organization moved slowly; it was February 20, 1865, before the first fifteen students entered the Institute. By grants of land the Commonwealth induced educational institutions to settle in the new Back Bay. Thus the Boston Society of Natural History in the course of the war began to build a museum on Berkeley Street between Boylston and Newbury streets. The remainder of the block having been granted to the Massachusetts Institute of Technology, a building was begun there in 1863, which, however, was only completed for full occupancy in 1866.

The new Institute building housed under one roof class rooms, laboratories, and offices; its great lecture room—92 by 65 feet and two stories high—long accommodated the Lowell Institute series and even provided a pulpit for Phillips Brooks during the four years between the burning of old Trinity Church in Summer Street and the completion of the present one in Copley Square. Moreover, its architect, William G. Preston, produced a singularly handsome example of the Corinthian order according to Vignola that harmonized with the adjacent museum that he had designed for the Boston Society of Natural History. After the retirement of William Barton Rogers from the presidency of M.I.T., this building was named in his honor. The Rogers Building was for nearly seventy years a great ornament to the Back Bay and one of the most familiar points of reference in Boston.

As Charles W. Eliot, the first professor of analytical chemistry and metallurgy at M.I.T., became president of Harvard

University in 1869, the question of union between the oldest and the newest institutions of learning in Massachusetts soon arose. In 1870, as well as twice in the first quarter of the twentieth century, the possibility of a merger with Harvard was fully explored and discarded in each instance. Thus the Massachusetts Institute of Technology developed as a completely independent organization, steadily growing in scientific resources decade by decade. And as its graduates rose to positions of respect and influence throughout American industry, it came to be thought of not as "Boston Tech" but as a scientific university of national utility.

In 1883 a new building, later named in honor of President Francis A. Walker, was completed beside the Rogers building, thus using all the ground available in the original grant from the Commonwealth. As the Back Bay offered no adequate land for future expansion, the Institute, by the beginning of the twentieth century, was seriously concerned about its future development. A site on the Cambridge shore of the Charles River Basin, near the Harvard Bridge, seemed ideal for size, accessibility, and dignity of setting, yet the financial problems of creating a wholly new campus there were great. Through the gift of half a million dollars in 1911 by T. Coleman du Pont, an alumnus of the Class of 1884, the first steps were taken. George Eastman of Rochester, by successive gifts to the Institute (of which he was not a graduate), presented nearly twenty million dollars and assured the completion of the project.

Thus in 1916, just fifty years after the occupancy of the Rogers Building, the Massachusetts Institute of Technology moved to Cambridge to a handsome complex of new buildings, designed by W. Welles Bosworth, that were reflected in the waters of the Charles River Basin. Until 1938 the department of architecture remained in the Rogers Building, but since that date M.I.T. has been entirely based in Cambridge. With the great expansion of its defense and other government activities during and since World War II, most of the Cambridge shore of the Basin from the Longfellow Bridge almost to the Boston University Bridge has become an M.I.T. preserve.

Striking evidence of Boston's commitment to learning in the second half of the nineteenth century is furnished by the number of men totally lacking in formal education who contributed generously towards the establishment of new colleges designed to broaden the opportunities of those who came after them. The Medford farmer and brickmaker Charles Tufts (1781–1876), a devout Universalist, gave twenty acres of his farm on the Medford-Somerville line for an institution that was incorporated in 1852 as Tufts College. Although the medical and dental schools that were established in the nineties were located in Boston, for proximity to hospitals, the other branches of Tufts College—liberal arts colleges for men and women, a college of engineering, graduate school of arts and sciences, and the Fletcher School of Law and Diplomacy—have remained on the Medford hillside given by Charles Tufts. In 1955 the name Tufts University was adopted in belated recognition of what the institution had actually been for well over half a century.

The establishment of Boston University in 1869 was chiefly due to three other New Englanders with no more formal schooling than Charles Tufts: Lee Claflin (1791–1871), a

Hopkinton tanner who expanded his business into making boots and shoes, Isaac Rich (1801–72), a Wellfleet boy who came to Boston peddling fish, and Jacob Sleeper (1802–89), a native of Newcastle, Maine, who prospered in the manufacture of ready-made clothing. All three were staunch Methodists and officers of the Boston Theological Seminary, which in 1871 became the first department of the new university. Within two years, schools of liberal arts, law, music, oratory, and medicine were created.

Boston University began life in the very heart of the city, for in 1869 the secretary of its trustees was based in the Old State House—not then restored—while Jacob Sleeper, the treasurer, had his office on the second floor of the Old Corner Bookstore building. The former buildings of the Baptist church on Somerset Street and of the Mount Vernon Place Congregational Church in Ashburton Place were adapted for academic use, while Isaac Rich bought the site of Bishop Cheverus' cathedral in Franklin Street as an investment for the university. From this early roost on the top of Beacon Hill, Boston University gradually proliferated departments over the city, wherever vacant buildings could be found, until in the nineteen thirties President Daniel L. Marsh began to create a central campus between Commonwealth Avenue and the Charles River Basin, near the Cottage Farm Bridge (now renamed in honor of the university). Gradually more and more departments have been drawn to new buildings there, while many private houses and apartments from Charlesgate along Bay State Road—not to forget the Braves Field in Commonwealth Avenue—have been converted to the uses of the university.

Another wholesale clothier, John Simmons (1796–1870), a native of Little Compton, Rhode Island, left trusts that led to the establishment in 1902 of Simmons College. This institution, which built in the Fenway near the Isabella Stewart Gardner Museum, was, as its first president, Henry Lefavour, remarked on its opening, "unique, in that it is the first to stand in New England for a utilitarian education for girls, while aiming not to neglect any influence that may broaden the students' outlooks and deepen their lives." From the first, the organization of the Simmons curricula was that of a technical institute with schools of household economics, secretarial studies, library science, general science, and social work for undergraduates.

Northeastern University, founded in 1898, states its flexible aim as the "discovery of community educational needs and the meeting of these in distinctive and serviceable ways." It offers instruction in liberal arts, education, business administration, engineering, and pharmacy, and through its co-operative plan a student may alternate terms of study with work at an outside job. Thus a possibility of higher education reaches many young people who might otherwise not get to college. Like Boston University on the Charles River, Northeastern University is creating a central campus with some dormitories on Huntington Avenue, midway between Symphony Hall and the Museum of Fine Arts. However, most of their students do not live at either of these large universities but commute to them from distant towns.

While Boston University owed its origin to three Methodist laymen, Boston College had been founded six years earlier by an Irish-born Jesuit, the Reverend John McElroy (1782–1877), who, after serving as a chaplain in the Mexican War, had come to Boston in 1847 to take charge of St. Mary's Church in the North End. Recognizing the need of higher education for the rapidly increasing Catholic population of Boston, Father McElroy, after unsuccessfully seeking a site in the West End for a Jesuit church and college, bought land on Harrison Avenue in the South End in 1857. Here he built the Church of the Immaculate Conception and the buildings in which Boston College, incorporated on April 1, 1863, opened to students in 1864. Father McElroy's chief lay backer in the early stages of the establishment of the college was Andrew Carney, founder of the Carney Hospital in South Boston, who had prospered in the wholesale clothing business in partnership with the Methodist Jacob Sleeper, soon to become a founder of Boston University.

After fifty years in the South End, Boston College moved to its present dramatic location in Chestnut Hill, overlooking the reservoir, where it is in close proximity to the Archbishop's House and to St. John's Seminary. In the nineteen twenties and thirties a Graduate School, Law School, School of Social Work, and College of Business Administration were created. Since 1954 the Boston Citizen Seminars on the fiscal, economic, and political problems of Boston and the metropolitan community, conducted by the College of Business Administration, have had a vital place in the life of the city as a whole, for they have brought together men of all groups—those who "own" the city and those who "run" it, as a journalist recently described them—for fruitful discussion of common problems.

Brandeis University in Waltham came into being in 1948 "because of the desire of American Jewry to make a corporate contribution to higher education in the tradition of the great American secular universities that have stemmed from denominational generosity." Although supported largely by Jewish generosity, the university's receptiveness to students of all faiths is indicated by the provision of Jewish, Catholic, and Protestant chapels. Brandeis, which calls itself "one of the few small universities in the United States," consists of a college and a graduate school of arts and sciences, as well as a graduate school for advanced studies in social welfare. It takes justifiable pride in the fact that only thirteen years after its founding it was authorized to establish a Phi Beta Kappa chapter.

Universalists, Methodists, Catholics, and Jews have thus all made their contributions to the creation of colleges and universities in metropolitan Boston. In addition to those already mentioned there are besides a bewildering number of theological schools, junior colleges, and colleges specializing in some professional training. One can most easily see the commitment of Boston to higher education by following the Charles River from the Longfellow Bridge toward Cambridge. Boston University is on the left bank; M.I.T. on the right; Harvard on both. The buildings of these institutions have not yet coalesced, but as all three have lately been seized with a mania for concrete towers, there is scarcely a spot along the river bank free from sight of something belonging to one of them.

IX

Hearing

FOR TALKING, thinking, reading, seeing, and learning, Boston's resources are richer and wider than for hearing. Instrumental and choral music flourish in abundance, but the opera has never been completely at home nor has the theater been much happier or more permanent. The reputation of Boston as a musical center rests most firmly upon the Boston Symphony Orchestra, which was, as has been noted in Chapter II, the personal and generous creation of a single State Street investment banker.

Henry Lee Higginson, born in 1834, entered Harvard College in 1851 but withdrew before the end of his freshman year because of weak eyesight. Having been sent to Europe for his health, the eighteen-year-old boy hived up in Dresden, hired a piano, and undertook to perfect both his knowledge of German and of music. Returning to Boston, but not to Harvard, he spent an interlude as a clerk in an India Wharf counting house before going back to Vienna to devote several years to the conscientious study of music. In the winter of 1860–61, Henry Higginson came home, and before he had settled in any regular occupation found himself caught up in the Civil War. By May 11, 1861, he was a second lieutenant in Company D of the Second Massachusetts Regiment, which two months later moved south to the front. In October, 1861,

Higginson was transferred to the new First Massachusetts Cavalry, with the rank of captain. In the spring of 1862 he was promoted to major. After service in South Carolina and in the Army of the Potomac under McClellan, Burnside, and Hooker, including the battles of Antietam and Chancellorsville, Major Higginson was severely wounded in an action at Aldie Gap, Virginia, on June 17, 1863. During a long convalescence in Boston, he married Louis Agassiz's daughter, Ida, on December 5, 1863.

Although Major Higginson attempted to return to active service in July, 1864, his injuries forced his resignation from the Army. Having by then a family to support, he experimented in Ohio oil fields and a Georgia cotton plantation for three years before entering the family firm of Lee, Higginson and Company at 44 State Street as a partner on January 1, 1868.

Thirteen years later, Henry Lee Higginson founded the Boston Symphony Orchestra, entirely on his own. His motives and methods are best understood by reading part of an address that he gave to the musicians of the orchestra on April 27, 1914, in his eightieth year:

"Gentlemen:

"Some years ago I wished to be a musician, and therefore went to Vienna, where I studied two years and a half diligently, learned something of music, something about musicians, and one other thing—that I had no talent for music. I heard there and in other European cities the best orchestras, and much wished that our own country should have such fine orchestras. Coming home at the end of 1860, I found our country in trouble, and presently in a great war. Naturally I took part in the war, at the end of which time I did various things, and at last came to our present office in State Street, where I was admitted as a partner.

"For many years I had hard work to earn my living and support my wife. Originally I had had a very small sum of money, which had been used up while studying in Vienna and during the war. All these years I watched the musical conditions in Boston, hoping to make them better. I believed that an orchestra of excellent musicians under one head and devoted to a single purpose could produce the results, and wished for the ability to support such an undertaking, for I saw that it was impossible to give music at fair prices and make the Orchestra pay expenses.

"After consulting with some European friends, I laid out a plan, and at the end of two very good years of business began concerts in the fall of 1881. It seemed best to undertake the matter single-handed, and, beyond one fine gift from a dear friend, I have borne the costs alone. All this is a matter of record, yet it may interest you. It seemed clear that an orchestra of this size and under possible conditions would cost at least $20,000 a year more than the public would pay. Therefore, I expected this deficit each year, and faced contracts with seventy men and a conductor. It was a large sum of money, which depended on my business each year and on the public. If the concert halls were filled, that would help me; if my own business went well, that would help me; and the truth is, that the great public has stood by me nobly.

"In my eyes the requisites about the Orchestra were these: to leave the choice and care of the musicians, the choice and care of the music, the rehearsals and direction of the Orchestra, to the conductor, giving him every power possible; to leave to an able manager the business affairs of the enterprise; and on my part, to pay the bills, to be satisfied with nothing short of perfection, and always to remember that we were seeking high art and not money; art came first, then the good of the public, and the money must be an after consideration."

Note particularly the last paragraph. How few patrons anywhere ever have combined with real generosity such modest self-abnegation and such an understanding of the means by which the highest artistic results are produced. Yet Major Higginson not only set such a standard in 1881 but scrupulously adhered to it until his death in 1919. In the years between 1881 and 1914, the aggregate deficit was at least $900,000, which Major Higginson cheerfully supplied. Such was the cost of high standards requiring frequent rehearsals by regularly employed musicians.

In the early nineteen thirties, while living in Barcelona, I sometimes attended symphony concerts at the Palau de la Musica Catalana. These were conducted by Pablo Casals, who came annually from France for a short season. Notwithstanding the distinction of the conductor, these performances were a lamentable contrast to what I had earlier known in Boston. The reason was simple. The season was brief and supported only by gate receipts. The rest of the year the musicians gave lessons, played in cafés, or otherwise scraped up a penny by any means they could. When Casals arrived, he rounded up his troops, with little opportunity for rehearsal or the development of that precision that can only come from repeated association. Now symphonic music in Boston before Major Higginson's generous advent was no better than in Barcelona thirty-five years ago; probably it was considerably worse.

Colonial Boston was hardly a propitious field for music. Puritans sang, sometimes accompanied by instruments, both in and out of church, but when in 1713, Thomas Brattle bequeathed a pipe organ to the Brattle Street Church, provided that they "procure a sober person that can play skilfully thereon with a loud noise," his benefaction was rejected. The Anglican King's Chapel, however, having less austere notions about the conduct of divine service, gratefully accepted the instrument. A certain number of music teachers offered their services in the advertisements of eighteenth-century Boston newspapers. From singing classes, such as that organized in Stoughton after the Revolution by William Billings, the first local composer of hymn tunes, evolved in 1815 the Handel and Haydn Society, which has continued uninterruptedly as a volunteer chorus for a century and a half. Although that society in 1823 thought sufficiently well of contemporary music to offer Beethoven a commission to write an oratorio for its use, Handel's *Messiah* has always been its favorite presentation.

The undergraduate Pierian Sodality, organized at Harvard College in 1808 to present orchestral music, proved so congenial a body that, at Commencement, 1837, a group of its former members who had been graduated founded the Harvard Musical Association to continue in Boston the musical pleasures of Cambridge. Incorporated in 1845, with headquarters in Boston, the Harvard Musical Association provided both a haven for the musically minded and some of the earliest chamber concerts in the city. It still functions, in a pleasant club house on Beacon Hill at 57A Chestnut Street, corner of West Cedar Street. Through the *Journal of Music*, edited from 1852 to 1881 by John Sullivan Dwight (Harvard, 1832), long its leading spirit, the Association profoundly influenced musical taste in Boston. It had, moreover, a considerable part in the construction of the Music Hall in Hamilton Place in 1852, "from which time forward," as M. A. De Wolfe Howe remarked, "it was unnecessary to ask a visiting Jenny Lind to sing in the Fitchburg Railroad Station." The Music Hall, which had been equipped in 1863 with a great German organ, provided ample space for orchestral music by various groups. In 1866 the Harvard Musical Association inaugurated a series of concerts, with an orchestra of fifty local musicians, that continued for some seventeen years.

It was, in fact, a concert of the Harvard Musical Association that provided Major Higginson with the conductor who was to be the key for his great design. On March 3, 1881, George Henschel, a visiting thirty-one-year-old German composer, singer, and teacher, conducted the first performance of his own Concert Overture at the last concert of the Harvard Musical Association's sixteenth series. The vigor, power, and effectiveness of his performance caused Major Higginson to send for him. Of the interview that followed, Sir George Henschel later recalled: "At that meeting Mr. Higginson revealed to me his plan of founding a new orchestra in Boston, and asked me if eventually I would undertake to form such an orchestra and conduct a series of concerts with it; adding that of course he quite understood singing to be a more lucrative thing than conducting so that, as—if I accepted—I could not earn as much money by singing as if I were free, he would make my salary such as to make it worth my while. I would be absolutely my own master, no one would interfere with my programme-making—there would, in fact, be no committee, etc."

Henschel was interested. Within a fortnight he accepted, and on March 30, Major Higginson sent to the Boston newspapers the first public announcement of his plan, which involved twenty concerts, to be given in the Music Hall on Saturday evenings from mid-October to mid-March, with reserved seats at modest prices. In addition, there would be a public rehearsal one afternoon of every week, with twenty-five cent unreserved seats.

To provide for the extended rehearsals that would be essential for the success of the plan, Major Higginson acquired control of the Music Hall. When tickets were placed on sale in the autumn, there was an amazing demand for them. Seventy-five people were in line at 6 A.M., some having been there all night. Thus on Saturday evening, October 22, 1881, the first season opened with a crowded and enthusiastic house. By the end of the first season, it was clear that Major Higginson had established a permanent orchestra, which required, and paid for, the exclusive services of its members for the greater part of four days each week during the season.

The twenty concerts and rehearsals of the first season were attended by 83,359 persons, the average total for each program being 4,168. In the second season, when the number of concerts was increased to twenty-six, the total attendance was 111,775, with an average of 4,299 at each. Moreover, six concerts were given for Harvard University at the Sanders

Theatre in Cambridge, and three each in Salem, Providence, and Worcester; two each in Portland, Lowell, Fitchburg, and New Bedford, and one each in Newport and Lynn. These fifty-two concerts in a single season both extended the scope of the orchestra and greatly increased its deficit; they also emphasized that it had become a continuing institution.

Henschel conducted the Boston Symphony Orchestra for three years. Although his friend Brahms, enchanted with the organization of an orchestra in which the conductor ruled supreme, unimpeded by committees, wrote him, "There's not a *Kapellmeister* on the whole of our continent who would not envy you that," Henschel returned to the European concert stage in 1884. His successor, Wilhelm Gericke (1884–89) had for ten years conducted the orchestra of the Vienna Court Opera before coming to Boston. During his tenure new and superior musicians were imported from Europe. To stabilize their employment by lengthening the season, trips to Philadelphia, New York, and St. Louis were inaugurated, as well as a series of Popular Concerts—soon abbreviated to Pops—in the early summer.

Although Gericke gave up the conductorship in 1889 after five years, he returned to Boston in 1898 for a second term, lasting until 1906. During his absence his place was filled successively by two conductors from the Stadt Theater of Leipzig, Arthur Nikisch (1889–93) and Emil Paur (1893–98). In 1893, just as Nikisch was leaving, the continued existence of the Music Hall was threatened by a city proposal for the construction of a new street through its site. When Major Higginson let it be known that, unless Bostonians cared enough for the Boston Symphony concerts to assure a proper building for their continuance, they would come to an end, a corporation was promptly formed to raise $400,000 to provide an acceptable substitute for the Music Hall. By November, 1893, it was announced that McKim, Mead and White—the architects of the Boston Public Library, then under construction in Copley Square—had begun plans for the new concert hall.

By the nineties the Back Bay, the filling of which had begun just before the Civil War, was substantially built up, and institutions in search of new space were looking westward. Thus a site for the new hall was chosen—not very felicitously as far as the future development of the region was concerned—at the corner of Huntington and Massachusetts avenues. In the end, seven years passed before the Boston Symphony Orchestra moved to the new Symphony Hall. The panic of 1893 delayed construction. Fortunately, the immediate threat to the demolition of the Music Hall never materialized; indeed its shell still exists under the disguise of Loew's Orpheum movie house. By the time Symphony Hall was completed, it had cost more than three quarters of a million dollars. It was handsome and suitable for its purpose; the efforts of the stockholders who built it, who never received any profit from their investment, constituted a well-deserved tribute by friends and neighbors to the founder and sustainer of the Boston Symphony Orchestra.

The German and Austrian tradition that Major Higginson had come to know during his youth in Vienna dominated the Boston Symphony Orchestra through the years of World War I. In the autumn of 1906, Dr. Karl Muck, on leave from the Royal Opera House in Berlin, became conductor of the

Boston Symphony Orchestra. When recalled to Germany in 1908, he was succeeded by Max Fiedler of Hamburg, who continued until Muck returned in 1912 for a second term. This event gave great satisfaction, for soon after Muck's first arrival in Boston it had been observed that "Mr. Gericke left the Symphony Orchestra a perfect instrument; Dr. Muck has given it a living voice."

The outbreak of war in 1914 caused anxiety about the future of the orchestra, for Dr. Muck and a number of the musicians were in Europe at the time. They returned without incident, however, to open the 1914-15 season, and until well into the spring of 1917, Boston Symphony Orchestra concerts continued successfully. After the entry of the United States into the war, certain zealous patriots on the home front began to extend their hatred of Germany to German music and musicians. It was a difficult moment for Major Higginson. He had passed his eightieth birthday in 1914; his financial affairs had encountered heavy weather, and musically he saw no way of continuing the orchestra without Dr. Muck's able help. Late in March, 1918, the conductor was arrested and interned as an enemy alien. A month later, in his eighty-fourth year, Major Higginson turned over the Boston Symphony Orchestra to a board of trustees formed of younger like-minded friends. For more than thirty-seven years he had, single-handed, maintained his creation and brought it to perfection. His only regret was his inability to provide an endowment that would have continued his generosity long after his death.

In the autumn of 1918, Henri Rabaud came from the Paris Opera for a one year term as conductor, to be followed for five years by another French musician, Pierre Monteux. The

Russian Serge Koussevitzky came to the United States for the first time in 1924 as conductor of the Boston Symphony Orchestra and remained at its head for a full twenty-five years. The combination of his leadership with a responsible board of trustees and an able business management carried the orchestra through years of depression, unionization, increased costs, and a second war. In 1934—the centenary of Major Higginson's birth—the orchestra took title to Symphony Hall, and the Friends of the Boston Symphony Orchestra, now numbering some five thousand persons, was formed. Through Dr. Koussevitzky's enthusiasm the Berkshire Music Center, a summer home for the Boston Symphony Orchestra, was created at "Tanglewood" estate in Lenox, Massachusetts. Upon Dr. Koussevitzky's retirement in 1949, the French tradition returned with Charles Munch, who continued thirteen years. With the present conductor, Erich Leinsdorf, who has now completed three seasons, a Viennese is once more at home in Boston.

After eighty-four years—sixty-five of which have been spent in the noble and acoustically superb Symphony Hall—the Boston Symphony Orchestra has become as permanent and as fixed a point of municipal reference as the gold dome of Bulfinch's State House. It holds so a distinguished place among the great orchestras of the country and of the world that, as Michael Steinberg recently remarked, "Bostonians are apt to be surprised when it is pointed out how varied and how alive musical activities are here."

For more than half of its life the Boston Symphony Orchestra has, when choral assistance was required, drawn upon the Harvard Glee Club and the Radcliffe Choral Society. This association, which began in Dr. Karl Muck's time with a 1917 performance of Brahms' *Schicksalslied*, sprang from the remarkable achievement with undergraduate singers of one man, Archibald T. Davison (1883–1961), James Edward Ditson Professor of Music at Harvard University. "Doc" Davison, as he was affectionately and invariably called—contrary to all normal Harvard habits—was a brisk, ruddy, stocky, short-haired man who looked more like a football coach than the traditional stereotype of a musician. But musician he was, and teacher as well, of the highest degree.

The son of a Dorchester physician, "Doc" Davison attended the Boston Latin School before entering Harvard College in the Class of 1906. As an undergraduate he was a church organist and choirmaster and conducted the Dorchester Philharmonic Society and the Norfolk House Glee Club, as well as composing and conducting various shows for the Pi Eta Club. He was fond of recalling that the chairman of the Music Department told him in 1906 that he would have been graduated *summa cum laude* rather than *magna* had he not "wasted so much time on these frivolous productions." In 1908, after taking a Ph.D. in music—the second or third ever given by Harvard—with a thesis on "The Harmonic Contributions of Claude Debussy," the new "Doc" spent a year in Paris studying organ and composition with Charles Marie Widor. During this winter he sang in Widor's Bach Choir, of which Albert Schweitzer was then the accompanist. He could never forget the time when Widor remarked to him: "I can't teach today. I'm too depressed. I have just learned that Schweitzer is going to throw everything over and go to Africa as a medical missionary." On returning to the United

States in 1909 with the intention of making a career in a family clam-canning business in Nova Scotia, "Doc" Davison obligingly agreed to teach at Harvard as the Music Department was temporarily short-handed. He did so for the next forty-five years. Few men anywhere have been greater teachers or more widely loved.

Appointed University organist and choirmaster in 1910, he promptly banished Barnaby, Dykes, and Stainer from the repertory of Appleton Chapel. Similarly, when the Harvard Glee Club, established in 1858 to sing rounds, drinking ditties, and miscellaneous college songs, asked him in 1912 to act as their coach, radical changes soon occurred. Before anyone realized what was happening, "The bullfrog on the bank" had given way to Palestrina, Orlando Lasso, Vittoria, Purcell, Bach, Handel, Holst, and Vaughan Williams. This "batrachian bankruptcy"—a phrase that pleased Davison—led the Harvard Glee Club both to a divorce from the Banjo and Mandolin clubs and a new association with the Boston Symphony Orchestra. By simultaneous training of the Radcliffe Choral Society, he developed a skilful group of women singers who could, on occasion, join with the Glee Club to achieve a well-balanced chorus.

The association with the Boston Symphony that began with Karl Muck has continued with his successors. Pierre Monteux remarked: "I have heard choruses which can sing louder, but none that can sing better." When, in 1931, Leopold Stokowski invited the Harvard Glee Club to join his Philadelphia Orchestra in a stage performance of Stravinsky's *Oedipus Rex* at the Metropolitan Opera House in New York, Serge Koussevitzky exclaimed: "Aha, when he wants the finest chorus in

178

the world, he has to have *my* chorus." So over the years the Harvard Glee Club and the Radcliffe Choral Society have joined the Boston Symphony Orchestra in Symphony Hall for performances of Bach's Magnificat and B minor Mass, the St. John and St. Matthew Passions, Beethoven's *Missa solemnis* and Ninth Symphony, and Brahms' *Requiem*, just as they joined forces in Holy Cross Cathedral on January 19, 1964, to offer Mozart's Requiem for the repose of the soul of John F. Kennedy.

In the summer of 1921, at the invitation of the French government, "Doc" Davison took the Harvard Glee Club to Europe and gave twenty-three concerts in eight weeks in France, Italy, Germany, and Switzerland. Robert Tangeman, in a biographical sketch of Davison, remarked: "This was the first time a college glee club had been treated as a serious musical organization. No quarter was asked from or given by the European critics whose praise nevertheless was unanimous." And of his teaching Mr. Tangeman observed: "Doc felt deeply that in order to love good music students must be taught to sing it well and to live with it. His constant aim was to include as many students as possible in the Radcliffe Choral Society and the Harvard Glee Club."

So many students wanted to be included that standards were high and competition keen. Although they were too high and too keen for me to make the grade as a freshman in 1922, I had some consolation for this disappointment by gaining admission two years later to Music 3a, "Doc's" course on "The History and Development of Choral Music," which met in Paine Hall for lectures on Monday and Wednesday mornings, and on late Thursday afternoons, jointly with the

Radcliffe course—segregation was then strictly observed otherwise—for singing the works studied. After forty years I still marvel at the contagious quality of the instruction. A certain number of footballers who had wandered in in search of a "snap" remained to learn more than they had expected. "Doc," sitting at the piano, would detect incomprehension on certain faces. Stopping his lecture, he would curse poetically under his breath for a moment, before repeating in simpler terms what he had just said. This process continued until every last man understood, and appreciated, what he was trying to explain.

Too often ability, enthusiasm, and patience of this kind prove to be individual possessions that cannot readily be duplicated. Fortunately for music at Harvard and in Boston there has been a kind of apostolic succession. When "Doc" Davison resigned as conductor of the Harvard Glee Club in 1933, he was succeeded by the equally beloved G. Wallace Woodworth, of the Class of 1924, who had followed the same road as University organist and professor of music. "Woody" continued "Doc's" basic policies, while adding new features of his own, over the next fifteen years. "Woody's" successor, Elliot Forbes, of the Class of 1941, returned to Harvard in 1958 as professor of music and director of the Harvard Glee Club and Radcliffe Choral Society after eleven years of teaching music at Princeton. With such a sequence of contagious conductors and teachers of music, choral singing has become an enduring part of the lives of thousands of men and women who have passed through Harvard and Radcliffe in the last half century. Some of those who remain in Boston after graduation continue their enthusiasm in the Chorus pro Musica, vigorously and imaginatively led by Alfred Nash Patterson, or in other of the choral groups that abound in the region.

At the dedication of the War Memorial Auditorium in the Prudential Center on February 24, 1965, the Harvard Glee Club, the Radcliffe Choral Society, and the Chorus pro Musica joined with the Boston University Chorus, the venerable Handel and Haydn Society, the M.I.T. Choral Society and Glee Club, and the New England Conservatory Chorus, in a program that combined Haydn, Mozart, Bach, Verdi, and Handel with the work of three contemporary Boston composers. The Handel and Haydn Society alone presented Mabel Daniels' *A Psalm of Praise*, while the combined choruses sang Randall Thompson's *Alleluia* and Daniel Pinkham's *Canticle of Praise*, commissioned especially for the occasion by Mayor John F. Collins.

Two nights earlier, the Boston Pops Orchestra had given a dedicatory concert under the direction of Arthur Fiedler, who has been its conductor since 1930. The Pops concerts, given by members of the Boston Symphony Orchestra in Symphony Hall in the late spring after the conclusion of the regular season, go back to 1885. They are to the Boston Symphony, as David McCord has remarked, "as the better popular-priced books on the newsstands today are to their original editions." When the Pops season is over, some of its players move to the Hatch shell by the Charles River for a series of out-of-door Esplanade Concerts.

Chamber music abounds in Boston, both with professional and amateur performers. Members of the Boston Symphony Orchestra participate in the Boston Symphony Chamber Players and in the Boston Symphony String Quartet, formerly designated the Nova Arte, which is based at the New England Conservatory of Music. Similarly, members of the Cambridge Festival Orchestra perform in the Fine Arts Wind Quartet. For some years the Camerata of the Museum of Fine Arts has presented early music using the old instruments in the Leslie Lindsey Mason Collection which were assembled by the Reverend Francis W. Galpin early in this century and given to the museum in 1917 by William Lindsey in memory of his daughter who was lost in the sinking of the *Lusitania*. I remember with particular pleasure a concert of the Camerata a few years ago when the announced performers were delayed by foul weather. The audience was seated in the Tapestry Gallery at the Museum of Fine Arts. Daniel Pinkham appeared in full evening dress, explained that he was to substitute, hung his tail coat over the back of a chair, rolled up his sleeves and tuned the harpsichord. Having completed that necessary preliminary, he resumed his coat, bowed to the audience, and provided a superb evening of harpsichord music.

Boston enthusiasm for early chamber music is reflected in the number of harpsichords built in the city. As long ago as 1907 the Swiss instrument-maker Arnold Dolmetsch was brought here by a piano manufacturer. Many of the fifty harpsichords and clavichords that he built are still in use today. At the present time there are no less than three harpsichord makers in the vicinity of Boston: Frank T. Hubbard in Waltham, and William R. Dowd and Eric Herz in Cambridge. Donald Warnock, probably the only full-time professional lute-maker in the United States, has his workshop in Cambridge, while Frederick von Huene makes recorders in Waltham, and Charles B. Fisk of Gloucester and Fritz Noack of Andover are building pipe organs appropriate for baroque music. A Fisk three-manual mechanical action organ was installed last year in King's Chapel in Boston, where Daniel Pinkham is director of music.

Opera has always had harder sledding in Boston than symphonic, chamber, and choral music. Early in the present century a resident opera company was envisioned to enlarge the cultural offerings already available. In 1909 a Boston Opera House was built in Huntington Avenue, two blocks above Symphony Hall and diagonally across from the new home of the New England Conservatory of Music, which had been founded in the South End in 1867. Although music shops and piano dealers still congregate on Boylston Street, facing the Common, between Tremont Street and Park Square, the shift of the Boston Symphony Orchestra to Symphony Hall in 1900 created a new musical neighborhood in Huntington Avenue above Massachusetts.

The vast and gilded Boston Opera House was built to accommodate the Boston Opera Company, directed by Henry Russell, which had been organized in emulation of the Metropolitan in New York. But the experiment never worked. After five years the resident company disbanded, and although the Boston Opera House survived for several decades—with an occasional visit from the Metropolitan or other companies—it was demolished in 1957 to make way for the expansion of Northeastern University. Thereafter, the annual week's visit of the Metropolitan Opera Company, to achieve which the Boston Opera Association makes a stalwart financial effort, was staged in the Boston Music Hall (formerly the Metropolitan movie house) in Tremont Street until 1965 when the new War Memorial Auditorium was opened. Among its other good works, the Boston Opera Association raised over a third of a million dollars to equip this vast convention hall—with capacity of over five thousand—with the stage facilities necessary for the presentation of opera. Although performances will only be intermittent there, hope for the future of opera lies in Sarah Caldwell's Boston Opera group, which, in spite of insufficient funds and inadequate quarters in the Back Bay Theater on Massachusetts Avenue, has achieved remarkable performances. Of it Michael Steinberg has observed: "The Boston Opera represents Boston musical life at its best. It is not merely that the artistic level is high, but that everything is freshly considered. It is something uniquely ours, not a carbon copy or smudgy facsimile of opera as given elsewhere."

There are far fewer theaters in Boston than there were in my childhood. My mother used to take me as a boy to the Copley Theater, where Henry Jewett attempted to maintain a repertory company. The repertorial effort failed in 1930; even the Copley Theater has been demolished. The theater district, running along Tremont Street from the Boylston Street corner of the Common, has fallen on evil days. The buildings are still there, but only the Colonial, the Shubert, and the smaller Wilbur are legitimate rather than mechanical. Moreover, when they are used, it is chiefly for tryouts of what will later appear on Broadway. There is considerably more spark in two off-Broadway-type theaters—the Charles Playhouse in a made-over church in Warrenton Street, and the tiny Bostonian Playhouse at 1138 Boylston Street—and in the dramatic efforts of university students. Harvard's Loeb Drama

184

Center, completed in 1960, Brandeis University's Spingold Theater Arts Center, and the Boston University Theater on Huntington Avenue near Symphony Hall—built for Henry Jewett in 1925—offer fine facilities for student experimentation in drama.

Undergraduate inspiration is by no means confined to formal theaters. The Lowell House Musical Society at Harvard has for more than twenty-five years annually produced in the house dining hall, with a minimum of convenience and a maximum of imagination, an opera, usually of the seventeenth or eighteenth century. Purcell's *King Arthur*, Handel's *Semele*, and the like, have been presented there with freshness and spirit. The 1965 opera, *The Barber of Seville, or, The Useless Precaution*, composed in 1782 by the Neapolitan Giovanni Paisiello (1740–1816) while in the service of the Empress Catherine the Great, offered a variant of the Figaro theme, while simultaneously satirizing the unreadiness of undergraduate productions. At the appointed hour two Radcliffe girls in 1965 costume were ceremonially sweeping the stage and driving nails into scenery, while the actors only got into their costumes as the opera progressed. Such performances have a charm that soon becomes lost with increased professionalization.

X

Epilogue

AT THE END OF THE PREFACE I warned the reader that this book represented "one man's Boston." Limitations of space imposed by the series in which it appears, like those of my own knowledge and experience, prevent me from mentioning even briefly many institutions that help to make present-day Boston a center of civilization. Just as pilgrims of the ancient world journeyed to Epidaurus in search of healing, modern rulers from Sir Anthony Eden to King Saud have come to Boston, drawn by the skill of its physicians and surgeons. Entire books could be written upon the medical and scientific aspects of the city, but as this story cannot be compressed by me into a few pages, I can only refer the reader to David McCord's *The Fabrick of Man*, a historical sketch written for the fiftieth anniversary of the Peter Bent Brigham Hospital, in which he has concentrated his long-standing love affair with the city into an account of one great medical institution.

Even within the themes covered, the six preceding chapters make no pretension to the inclusiveness of an inventory or a guide book. *The Cultural Resources of Boston*, published in the spring of 1965 by the American Federation of Arts and the Institute of Contemporary Art to mark the occasion of the Fifty-first Biennial Convention of the Federation in Boston, is far more comprehensive in its listing, while a guide book to Boston that I am preparing for the Harvard University Press and the Modern Library will contain much information useful for reference that was necessarily excluded from this little book. My purpose in this essay has been simply to outline the interrelation between the past and present of Boston that has made it a center of civilization.

I have suggested earlier that the blending of scholars with an endlessly renewable supply of literate and responsible trustees and treasurers has done more than anything else to foster the institutions that, in Alfred North Whitehead's opinion, place Boston in a position comparable to that occupied by Paris in the middle ages. It is no exaggeration to claim that these universities and cultural institutions are the decisive factor in the present and future of the city. They draw potentially valuable people from all parts of the United States and many corners of the world, a number of whom stay here, not just to teach, but to practice law, medicine, or engage in business.

On February 23, 1965, in the course of the dedication of the city's War Memorial Auditorium, a seminar was held entitled "The New Bostonian, a symposium on the people behind the City of Ideas." Two of the participants who joined me in this discussion prove my point by their own choices of careers. Ephron Catlin, Jr., senior vice-president of the First National Bank of Boston, hails from St. Louis, but came to Harvard College with the Class of 1932. Eli Goldston arrived from Ohio a decade later as a Harvard undergraduate, remained to take graduate degrees in business administration and law, returned to Ohio to practice law for a time, and is now back in Boston as president of the Eastern Gas and Fuel Associates.

In the course of our discussion it was pointed out that the president of Harvard was born in Iowa, and that the heads of many other institutions and a multitude of Bostonians distinguished in professions first came here as students. Indeed, it became apparent how completely the Hudson River and the Alleghanies have ceased, like the Atlantic Ocean before them, to be effective barriers against the migration of peoples. Mr. Catlin suggested that, "If you took the various human ingredients that go towards creating a citizen of Boston and made a composite of them, you'd come up with somebody about forty years old, making about $5,000 a year. He would be mostly of Irish or Italian extraction: he'd have a fair bit of Russian blood in him and quite a few relatives in Canada. He'd be about 10 per cent Negro and he would probably have a little Yankee blood in him. He might be named Erastus O'Callahan Pellegrini Lowellski."

Although this is entirely plausible so far as statistics are concerned, you will no more find Mr. Catlin's "Erastus O'Callahan Pellegrini Lowellski" in the Boston telephone book today than you would have found the late John P. Marquand's "George Apley" a generation ago. Such composites, plausible as they seem, remain in the realm of literary inspiration, for most Bostonians, whatever their origin or whenever they appeared on the scene, remain individualists. In Boston even newspapers, which in many cities present a visage of composite conformity, harbor individualists like the late Lucien Price of the *Boston Globe* and the happily-still-thriving Francis W. Dahl, whose inimitable cartoons have appeared on the editorial page of the *Boston Herald* since 1930.

Lucien Price, born in Kent, Ohio, in 1883, came to Harvard

in the Class of 1907. In the autumn of 1914 he joined the staff of the *Globe*, where for the next fifty years he wrote editorials in which the most elevated thoughts of classical Greece, of Goethe, and of Alfred North Whitehead were brought to bear upon contemporary problems, in beautiful language which any reader could understand. He loved music, mountains, the sea, the English language, human integrity and courage; with equal fervor he hated war, injustice, sham, and unkindness. To me, Lucien Price always seemed a teacher without a classroom; a peripatetic philosopher whose Lyceum embraced the mountains of Greece and Vermont, the shores of Nova Scotia and Nahant, the battlefield of Chaeronea, the sidewalks of Beacon Hill—where he lived simply in a couple of rooms at 75 Hancock Street—and, now and then, my office at the Boston Athenaeum. Shortly before his death in the spring of 1964, he gave the Athenaeum the scrapbooks in which he had mounted clippings of his editorials over the previous half-century. Only when one saw these lapidary pieces together could one realize the contribution that he had made to the intellectual life of Boston over this long period.

Francis W. Dahl for thirty-five years has commented with oblique and penetrating wit upon happenings of the day in cartoons that consist usually of six consecutive boxes of drawings following the quotation of a recent news item. He is good humored, understated, imaginative, and, above all, timely, for his drawings normally represent a flight of fancy based upon some absurdity in the news of the previous day. *The New Yorker* quotes some ridiculous bit of Americana (in the H. L. Mencken sense) and make it unforgettable by a few carefully chosen words that follow, but there are always some days, if not some weeks, between the text and sermon. Working for a daily newspaper, Dahl's wit has to be almost instantaneous, for an absurdity of Monday frequently meets its comeuppance on Tuesday morning. Several books of his drawings have been published. It is good to have them available, but it is even better to open the *Herald* each morning to see what he has devised.

In the past decade the service of the Boston and Maine Railroad has been steadily and inexorably deteriorating. I like trains, and regard them as the only rational means for getting in and out of a city. If I am to stick by this conviction and avoid traffic jams, I must now present myself at the Andover station at 7:35 A.M., for there is now no other train. It is a bit of a travesty to speak of the "Andover station," for the Boston and Maine Railroad, in its eagerness to discourage passengers, has sold that building to a firm that deals in lawnmowers. There is no ticket office, no proper waiting room; only a crossing-tender with a symbolical red flag, and a platform, left over from better days, from which, on a winter day, one wades through the snow to board the only train. This descent into indecency inspires gloomy reflections each morning, yet when I am on the train and open the *Boston Herald*, Dahl—like our flag—is still there, and I feel better about the world.

Dahl's satire is invariably amusing; sometimes it achieves public benefits that could hardly be obtained by reasoned argument or solemn denunciation. A few years ago, just as I was about to take a plane to Virginia, a lady in Commonwealth Avenue telephoned me to pour out her sorrows concerning whitewashed rocks recently placed along walks in the Public Garden, and hoped that I could do something about getting them removed. After explaining that I had not seen them and was on the point of departure, I further suggested that, as they doubtless represented a sincere desire on the part of some municipal employee to improve the appearance of the Garden, it would be awkward to rush forward with denunciations of his lack of taste; nevertheless, I would see what I could do. In the few minutes that remained before going to Logan Airport, I sent Dahl a postcard reporting the conversation. When I returned some days later, I found on my desk three items: (a) a card from Dahl saying he would do what he could; (b) a cartoon from the next day's *Herald* in which he unforgettably reduced the rocks to an absurdity, and (c) a telephone message from my informant in Commonwealth Avenue expressing pleasure that they had been removed. Thanks to Dahl, I was spared ever seeing those rocks.

Thirty-five years ago, Samuel Eliot Morison placed on the title page of his *Builders of the Bay Colony* a line of Horace: "*Quamquam ridentem dicere verum, quid vetat?*" Indeed, as Mr. Morison's books over the past fifty years so strikingly demonstrate, the truth is usually better conveyed with a smile than by a solemn harangue. Francis W. Dahl works on the same principle in his cartoons. Similarly, in verse sometimes set to music, Francis W. Hatch copes with the absurdities of contemporary Boston.

In 1957, when a ridiculous proposal was made to throw the butchers out of Faneuil Hall to make way for tourist trade "gifte shoppees," Frank Hatch's ballad "Beef before Baubles," printed as a broadside that passed from hand to hand in the eighteenth-century manner, brought matters back into focus.

This lively verse, which describes the delights of buying bacon, broiler, tripe, and cheese in Faneuil Hall, concludes with the ringing verses:

Bestir ye!
Peter Faneuil,
Old Frenchman in your grave,
'Twas not for tourist folderol
Your deed of trust you gave.

You planned and gave
A Market Hall
Designed for honest trade,
With quarters up above, where men
Could call a spade a spade.

Here orators
In ages past
Have mounted their attack
Undaunted by proximity
Of sausage on the rack.

Here men have shouted,
Age on age,
With fervor for their cause,
And, going home, bought nourishment
To steel a freeman's jaws.

Let tourists come,
Let tourists go
And carry home belief
That Boston Patriots are backed
By honest Yankee beef!

Enlarging upon this theme in an editorial in *The Pilot*, Monsignor Francis J. Lally intimated that the idea of separating the market from Faneuil Hall—"brought in by gypsies we must imagine"—"might not end till the most awful things had happened. After Faneuil Hall is 'cleaned up' for the tourist trade, they would wrap the old State House in cellophane and then, we suppose, laminate the gold dome of the new one. Before we knew it we would have a rotary around the 'massacre site' and even the tramps would be thrown off the Common.

"This may be fine for those who feel some interest in the past but really have no sense of history. For the rest of us it is nonsense. Old things, full of memory, should not be sterilized, polished and wrapped as if to make of the city some precious antiseptic museum."

It used to be said that the indispensible attributes of a proper Bostonian were a share in the Athenaeum, a lot in Mount Auburn Cemetery, and a relative in the McLean Asylum at Waverley. In concluding this editorial, Monsignor Lally proposed a new and more agreeable triad, in this form: "Just as long as men buy beef at Faneuil Hill, and men take books from the Boston Athenaeum, and lunch is served at Locke-Ober's—Boston and our city and our country will be better for it."

The most vivid impressions of Boston yet recorded are in David McCord's *About Boston: Sight, Sound, Flavor & Inflection*, now seventeen years old but going strong in paperback, as good as ever. He is a Bostonian by choice and conviction rather than inertia, for his Pennsylvania family was of Scottish origin and he was born in New York. Coming to

Harvard in the Class of 1921, he chose to remain here, and, although he has worked for the university for more than forty years, has lived almost as long on the shady side of Commonwealth Avenue in Boston. The last essay in *About Boston* is a litany of the things that David McCord likes about the city. It is too long to be quoted, too good to be excerpted. Therefore I can only refer my readers to it, and add that a thing that I particularly like about Boston is the presence of men like McCord, Morison, Lally, Hatch, and Dahl, who combine wit and style in whatever they do. So for that matter did John Fitzgerald Kennedy.

Suggested Reading

THE FOLLOWING PARAGRAPHS are in no sense a bibliography. They simply contain suggestions for readers who may wish to know more about the history of Boston. In them will be found a mixture of scholarly monographs, books written for a wider audience, biographies, autobiographies, and even some novels. Most of them are pleasant reading for one reason or another; all of them convey something about Boston as a place and the people who have made it what it is.

Of the innumerable works of the historian Samuel Eliot Morison, the following are particularly relevant: *Builders of the Bay Colony* (Boston, Houghton Mifflin Company, 1930, reprinted in Sentry Books 32), *The Intellectual Life of Colonial New England* (New York, New York University Press, 1956, reprinted in paperback), *Three Centuries of Harvard 1636–1936* (Cambridge, Harvard University Press, 1936), *The Maritime History of Massachusetts* (Boston, Houghton Mifflin Company, 1921, reprinted in Sentry Books 6), *The Life and Letters of Harrison Gray Otis, Federalist, 1765–1848* (Boston, Houghton Mifflin Company, 1913), *By Land and By Sea* (New York, Alfred A. Knopf, 1953), *The Parkman Reader* (Boston, Little, Brown and Company, 1955), and *One Boy's Boston 1887–1901* (Boston, Houghton Mifflin Company, 1962).

Carl Bridenbaugh in *Cities in the Wilderness: The First Century of Urban Life in America, 1625–1742* (New York, Alfred A. Knopf, 1955, reprinted in Capricorn Books 242) and *Cities in Revolt, Urban Life in America, 1743–1775* (New York, Alfred A. Knopf, 1955, reprinted in Capricorn Books 243) compares the evolution of colonial Boston with that of Newport, New York, Philadelphia, and Charleston. Boston is one of the sixteen cities considered in Constance McLaughlin Green's *American Cities in the Growth of the Nation* (London, Athlone Press, 1957, reprinted in Harper Colophon Books CN 61K).

My *Boston: A Topographical History* (Cambridge, Belknap Press of Harvard University Press, 1959), deals with the physical appearance of the place over three centuries. *Boston: Portrait of a City* (Barre, Mass., Barre Publishers, 1964), in which I wrote a text to elucidate Katharine Knowles's photographs, illustrates the present appearance. David McCord's *About Boston* (Garden City, Doubleday and Co., 1948; reprinted by Little, Brown Company in paperback, 1964) should be read for reasons that I suggested at the end of the epilogue.

Five of the books of the Institute of Early American History and Culture at Williamsburg, all published at Chapel Hill by the University of North Carolina Press, are concerned with some aspect of Boston: Darrett B. Rutman, *Winthrop's Boston, A Portrait of a Puritan Town, 1630–1649* (1965); Emery Battis, *Saints and Sectaries, Anne Hutchinson and the Antinomian Controversy in the Massachusetts Bay Colony* (1962); Michael G. Hall, *Edward Randolph and the American Colonies, 1676–1703* (1960); John A. Schutz, *Wil-*

liam Shirley, King's Governor of Massachusetts (1961); and Carl Bridenbaugh, *Peter Harrison, First American Architect* (1949). Two Institute editions of eighteenth-century travelers' narratives contain attractive glimpses of the colonial town; Carl Bridenbaugh, ed., *Gentleman's Progress, the Itinerarium of Dr. Alexander Hamilton, 1744* (1948) and Howard C. Rice, Jr., ed., *Travels in North America in the Years 1780, 1781, and 1782 by the Marquis de Chastellux* (1963).

For the maritime beginnings of Boston, Bernard Bailyn's *The New England Merchants in the Seventeenth Century* (Cambridge, Harvard University Press, 1955) and *Massachusetts Shipping 1697–1714* (Cambridge, Belknap Press of Harvard University Press, 1959) are indispensible, as is Oscar Handlin, *Boston's Immigrants* (Cambridge, Belknap Press of Harvard University Press, 1959) for the nineteenth-century changes in population.

Ola Elizabeth Winslow, *Samuel Sewall of Boston* (New York, The Macmillan Company, 1964), Esther Forbes, *Paul Revere and the World he lived in* (Boston, Houghton Mifflin Company, 1942, reprinted in Sentry Books 21), and Clifford K. Shipton, *New England Life in the 18th Century* (Cambridge, Belknap Press of Harvard University Press, 1963) give excellent pictures of some colonial Bostonians. Any reader whose appetite is whetted by the third of these will wish to go on to Mr. Shipton's *Sibley's Harvard Graduates*, of which ten volumes have been published by the Harvard University Press between 1933 and 1965; these contain biographical sketches of graduates of Harvard College from the class of 1690 to that of 1755, many Bostonians among them.

For the local aspects of the American Revolution, see Benjamin W. Labaree, *The Boston Tea Party* (New York, Oxford University Press, 1964), Arthur Bernon Tourtellot, *William Diamond's Drum*, (Garden City, Doubleday and Company, Inc., 1959, reprinted as *Lexington and Concord, The Beginning of the War of the American Revolution* in the Norton Library N 194), and Douglas Southall Freeman, *George Washington, A Biography* (New York, Charles Scribner's Sons, 1948–57), Volume III, chapters 19–22, and Volume IV, chapters 1–3. Joseph G. E. Hopkins, *Patriot's Progress* (New York, Charles Scribner's Sons, 1961) is a plausible historical novel of the period.

Bostonians of the nineteenth and early twentieth centuries are well depicted in such varied works as Josiah Quincy, *Figures of The Past* (Boston, 1883, republished with an introduction by M. A. DeWolfe Howe by Little, Brown and Company in 1926); George Ticknor, *Life of William Hickling Prescott* (Boston, 1864); Robert Bennet Forbes, *Personal Reminiscences* (3rd ed., Boston, 1892); William Lawrence, *Memories of a Happy Life* (Boston, Houghton Mifflin Company, 1926); Edward Waldo Emerson, ed., *The Early Years of the Saturday Club, 1855–1870* (Boston, Houghton Mifflin Company, 1918); M. A. DeWolfe Howe, ed., *Later Years of the Saturday Club, 1870–1920* (Boston, Houghton Mifflin Company, 1927); Edward W. Forbes and John H. Finley, Jr., eds., *The Saturday Club, A Century Completed, 1920–1956* (Boston, Houghton Mifflin Company, 1958); Joseph F. Dineen, *The Purple Shamrock, The Hon. James Michael Curley of Boston* (New York, W. W. Norton and Company, 1949); and Mayor Curley's autobiography, *I'd do it again! A*

Record of All My Uproarious Years (Englewood Cliffs, Prentice-Hall, Inc., 1957). Five biographies by Louise Hall Tharp (all published by Little, Brown and Company) recreate very different types of local residents: *The Peabody Sisters of Salem* (1950), *Until Victory, Horace Mann and Mary Peabody* (1953), *Three Saints and a Sinner, Julia Ward Howe, Louisa, Annie and Sam Ward* (1956), *Adventurous Alliance, The Story of the Agassiz Family of Boston* (1959), and *Mrs. Jack, a Biography of Isabella Stewart Gardner* (1965). Three very lively books concerning Boston people appeared while this book was in press: Edward Chase Kirkland, *Charles Francis Adams, Jr., 1835–1915, The Patrician at Bay* (Cambridge, Harvard University Press, 1965); Helen Howe, *The Gentle Americans, 1864–1960, Biography of a Breed* (New York, Harper and Row, 1965); and Martin Green, *The Problem of Boston* (New York, W. W. Norton and Company, 1966). In William Dean Howells's *The Rise of Silas Lapham* and in the novels of John P. Marquand and Edwin O'Connor, fictional characters often behave exactly in the manner of genuine residents.

Francis Russell, in *Tragedy at Dedham* (New York, McGraw-Hill Book Company, 1962), and *The Great Interlude: Neglected Events and Persons from the First World War to the Depression* (New York, McGraw-Hill Book Company, 1964) revives often-forgotten incidents of the nineteen-twenties.

For further details on some Boston institutions see my *Boston Public Library: A Centennial History* (Cambridge, Harvard University Press, 1956), and *Independent Historical*

Societies (Boston, Boston Athenaeum, 1962), Stephen T. Riley, *The Massachusetts Historical Society, 1791–1959* (Boston, Massachusetts Historical Society, 1959), and David McCord, *The Fabrick of Man: Fifty Years of the Peter Bent Brigham* (Boston, Peter Bent Brigham Hospital, 1963).

Index